KU-324-506

WHITEHALL'S BLACK BOX

ACCOUNTABILITY AND PERFORMANCE IN THE SENIOR CIVIL SERVICE

GUY LODGE AND BEN ROGERS

ippr

The **Institute for Public Policy Research** (ippr) is the UK's leading progressive think tank and was established in 1988. Its role is to bridge the political divide between the social democratic and liberal traditions, the intellectual divide between academia and the policy making establishment and the cultural divide between government and civil society. It is first and foremost a research institute, aiming to provide innovative and credible policy solutions. Its work, the questions its research poses and the methods it uses are driven by the belief that the journey to a good society is one that places social justice, democratic participation and economic and environmental sustainability at its core.

For further information you can contact ippr's external affairs department on info@ippr.org, you can view our website at www.ippr.org and you can buy our books from Central Books on 0845 458 9910 or email ippr@centralbooks.com.

Our trustees

Chris Powell (Chairman)
Chai Patel (Secretary)
Jeremy Hardie (Treasurer)

Professor Kumar Bhattacharyya
Lord Brooke
Lord Eatwell
Lord Gavron
Professor Anthony Giddens
Lord Hollick
Jane Humphries
Roger Jowell
Neil Kinnock
Frances O'Grady

Carey Oppenheim
Sir Michael Perry
David Pitt-Watson
Dave Prentis
Lord Puttnam
Sir Martin Rees
Ed Sweeney
Baroness Williams
Baroness Young of Old Scone

© IPPR 2006

I am accountable to my own ideal of a civil servant.
Sir William Armstrong, Cabinet Secretary (speaking in the 1970s, cited in Chapman 1988)

Even Whitehall now accepts that Ministers cannot be accountable for everything. But the demise of one constitutional principle has not been matched by the development of another ... new ways are needed whereby officials can be called to account.
William Plowden (*Ministers and Mandarins* 1994)

Nothing can be easier than to make a case, as we may say, against any particular system, by pointing out with emphatic caricature its inevitable miscarriages, and by pointing out nothing else.
Walter Bagehot (*The English Constitution* 1867)

CONTENTS

About the authors

Guy Lodge is a Research Fellow in the democracy team at ippr. He specialises in governance and constitutional reform and has published widely in this area. Before joining ippr he worked at the Constitution Unit, in the School of Public Policy, University College London. In 2005/06 Guy was also a Visiting Research Fellow in the Department of Politics and International Relations, University of Oxford.

Ben Rogers is an Associate Director of ippr and has been Director of its democracy team since 2004. He has a doctorate from Oxford in intellectual history and has written books on philosophy and history. He has researched and published on a range of topics at ippr, and has special interests in theories of social justice, civic life, local government and constitutional reform.

Acknowledgements

We would like to extend our thanks to all those who gave so much time to this project – at seminars, in conversation, and most of all those who agreed to be interviewed for the research, busy ministers and senior officials especially. We would also like to pay special thanks to the civil servants who have assisted us with research material for this project, especially those in the Cabinet Office who provided us with excellent and up-to-date data. It is, of course, a civil service convention – one we hope will change – that these people remain anonymous.

Very special thanks go to Susanna Kalitowski, whose hugely impressive and invaluable research support made this report and project possible.

At ippr, we would like to thank Holly Andrew, Richard Darlington, Ian Kearns, Emily Keaney, Georgina Kyriacou, Rick Muir, Nick Pearce and Lucy Stone.

We are also extremely grateful to a number of people who have helped throughout this project – by reading and commenting on drafts, or offering their thoughts more generally. These include Michael Barber, Michael Bichard, Vernon Bogdanor, Rupert Darwell, Andrew Gamble, Richenda Gambles, David Faulkner, Kate Jenkins, Iain Mclean, Jon Mendelsohn, Nick Montagu, Geoff Mulgan, Will Paxton, B. Guy Peters, David Pinto-Duschinsky, Nick Sharman, Martin Stanley, Graham Steel, Ed Straw, Colin Talbot and Diana Woodhouse.

We would also like to thank our principle funder, the Policy Network Foundation. Without its generous support this project would not have been possible. We are also grateful to the Campaign for Fair Taxation for funding a dedicated piece of work on HM Revenue and Customs.

What we heard

One thing is certain in Whitehall – the pace of change is slow. Especially when compared to parts of the private sector and local government. There is no agency for driving change. We develop our own reform programme and then are left to get on and implement it. (Permanent Secretary)

The most fundamental problem with the civil service is that it is not accountable to anybody. It is certainly not accountable to ministers. [This lack of accountability] explains why the pace of change in Whitehall is best described as glacial. (Minister)

Accountability is the central issue but it is difficult. The current arrangements are fraught with ambiguities – and remember this suits both sides. The accountability fudge we have now protects ministers and officials. Ministers can say "not me, guv" while officials hide behind them. This is not in the interest of effective government. (Senior official)

Is there a culture of ambition in Whitehall? I think this is the central issue for us and the jury is still out. (Permanent Secretary)

Why are we poor at delivery? Mainly it's because there aren't any rewards or sanctions for good delivery. (Senior official)

The Cabinet Secretary has no real power base in Whitehall. This is a major weakness. Because Permanent Secretaries are accounting officers in their own right there is no thick line of accountability between the Cabinet Secretary and Permanent Secretaries. This needs changing. Currently poor performers are eased out in a very traditional mandarin way. It's not an effective approach. I would like to see the Cabinet Secretary have the power to remove Permanent Secretaries. (Permanent Secretary)

As a group Permanent Secretaries have managed to duck accountability. A number of recent changes are beginning to change things but it needs to be made stronger. Permanent Secretaries should be held to account for making sure that their departments are 'fit for purpose', and that they have the right capabilities in place … we do need to find a mechanism for much greater and rigorous scrutiny of Permanent Secretary performance. I think it is very difficult to argue against the logic that this be a form of external scrutiny. (Permanent Secretary)

Although I think that the civil service is in a better shape than I have ever seen it in over thirty years, I would say that clarifying the role of ministers and officials is the major unresolved constitutional question. It is a question that has been deliberately left untouched – the Pandora's Box that now needs opening. (Permanent Secretary)

Whitehall's culture and way of thinking stems from its constitutional position and its relationship with ministers. ... You won't achieve significant reform unless the constitutional position of the service is addressed. (Senior official)

For some reason ministers never value the importance of civil service reform – it just isn't a priority and therefore the civil service is left to get on with things themselves. (Ex senior official)

Summary: Twelve propositions on civil service reform

1. The senior civil service is one of the most important institutions in the United Kingdom. No government of any colour will be able to achieve its aims without a high-performing civil service. This is particularly true of a government, like the present, that has made public service reform a priority.

2. The British civil service is admired throughout the world. It attracts an exceptionally high calibre of entrants; it has high standards of probity; the public it serves largely trusts it.

3. If an institution is under-performing, this is usually largely because of the way it is managed and governed, rather than because of any inadequacy in the people working for it.

4. Despite its qualities, the civil service is under-performing in key respects. It is often ineffective in carrying out its core functions of policy design and operational delivery. Too much Whitehall activity is undermined by its inability to work effectively across departmental boundaries; by a narrow skills-base; and under-developed leadership. It lacks a strong centre able to think strategically, manage civil service-wide change or drive standards up. Performance is poorly managed, and poor performance too often goes unchecked.

5. These weaknesses are not new and have long been recognised. Indeed, the civil service has been subject to a long succession of reforms, intended, but frequently failing, to address them.

6. The constitutional conventions governing the civil service and regulating its relationship with ministers, Parliament and the public are now anachronistic and severely inadequate. This is particularly true of the most important of these: the convention of ministerial responsibility. Together, these conventions entail that relations between ministers and civil servants are ill-defined, and their respective roles and responsibilities unclear. As a result, there is a 'governance vacuum' at the top of Whitehall: lines of accountability are confused and leadership is weak.

7. Many of the civil service's weaknesses are traceable to its inadequate system of governance and confused lines of accountability. They could be remedied by a better system.

8. Previous reform efforts have not addressed the inadequacy in the civil service's governance arrangements. Instead of seeking to reform the way the civil service is governed, they have focused on second order problems and left its constitutional conventions, and so its basic accountability structure, in place. That is why many of the problems

that they were meant to address persist.

9. Government should reform the governance system of the civil service as a priority. It needs, in particular, to recast the doctrine of ministerial responsibility.

10. There are, broadly, two options for reforming the way that Whitehall is held to account:

   ● Ministers could, as in the United States, make a 'reality' of ministerial responsibility by appointing senior civil servants. Ministers would then be responsible to Parliament, and ultimately the electorate, for every aspect of civil service performance.

   ● The convention of ministerial responsibility could be reformulated, making politicians responsible for 'policy' decisions and civil servants responsible for clearly defined 'operational' ones. Means would then have to be found to ensure that both were made properly accountable to Parliament and the public for the way in which they handle their responsibilities.

11. It is possible to combine elements of these two options. Nevertheless, the second is generally preferable. Britain already has a strong executive, and giving it further powers to appoint and dismiss civil servants would risk strengthening it further. Introducing a clearer division of responsibilities between ministers and mandarins and improving the arrangement by which both are held to account would improve government performance.

12. Both ministers and civil servants stand to gain from a greater demarcation of responsibilities. Civil servants will gain new responsibilities and a higher public profile. Ministers will get a professional, better managed, more strategic and outward-looking civil service. They will also get more support in making policy.

1 Introduction and overview

There is no more important organisation in the UK than the civil service. It is the engine of the British state. No government, of any political persuasion, can hope to achieve its aims without a well-run, high-performing civil service. This is perhaps particularly true of a government, like the present one, which has made public service reform a defining priority. But it is not just ministers who rely on the civil service. Local government, the National Health Service, schools, the police service, universities, the armed forces, the railway system, and the voluntary and private sectors all depend on it too. It shapes our lives – and life chances – in countless ways.

Yet, surprisingly, the civil service is often neglected and overlooked by politicians, commentators and the broader policy community. Though headlines are, as we write, dominated by crises at the Home Office and elsewhere in Whitehall,[1] it is rare for Whitehall to get serious, constructive attention from the political class. Two examples illustrate the point. In nine years as Prime Minister, Tony Blair has made just two speeches on the civil service, though he has made dozens of speeches on public service reform (Blair 1998; 2004). Labour's lengthy 2005 manifesto failed to mention the civil service once (Labour Party 2005).

This report explores some of the civil service's strengths and weaknesses and makes suggestions as to how it needs to change if it is to meet the challenges it faces. Continuing a line of ippr reports on the civil service (see Davies and Williams 1991; Plowden 1994; and Hunt 2001), it is based on a year-long research study that included the following components:

- Over 65 interviews with key Whitehall stakeholders. This consisted of 40 interviews with senior civil servants – including 10 Permanent Secretaries – and eight ministers. We also interviewed ex-civil servants, academics, special advisers, MPs, and leaders from the public, voluntary and private sectors. The interviews were conducted between March 2004 and February 2005. (Some of the people we spoke to have since moved post.)
- Extensive desk-based research and a literature review of the history of civil service reform and recent writings on government, governance and public management reform.
- Analysis of official documents, including some obtained uniquely by ippr under the Freedom of Information (FOI) Act.
- A series of ippr research seminars with experts from the UK and abroad.
- A focus group seminar with civil service fast streamers to test our analysis and findings.

- A research paper exploring international trends in civil service reform and relevant lessons from overseas, and a case study on HM Revenue and Customs. (ippr plans to publish separate reports on its international work and on the HMRC case study later this year.)

Note that all information hitherto referred to as (Cabinet Office/ippr) was provided to us by the Cabinet Office, and is available from ippr on request.

Our research focused on the senior civil service – the 'Whitehall Village' – and the senior civil servants who work in it (Heclo and Wildavsky 1981). Whitehall is by no means the same thing as the civil service. Indeed, if we define senior civil servants as grade 5 and above, then the senior civil service (SCS) comprises just 3,900 employees out of a total of half a million – less than one per cent of the civil service. Some critics might question whether we need 'another' focus on this cadre of mandarin. They have a point. The Whitehall *esprits de corps* have been the subjects of a disproportionate number of reports over the years, and there is need for research on the junior and middle ranking parts of the service and especially on the agencies. These have been seriously neglected.[2]

Nevertheless, we feel justified in focusing on the upper parts of the organisation, principally because of their importance in making the rest of the civil service – and beyond – work effectively. There are two further reasons. In many respects, the senior civil servants working at the heart of government have largely escaped systemic reform in the post-war period (Jenkins 2004). The Next Steps reforms, for instance, focused on the periphery, not the core (Talbot 2005). We also believe that changes within the operating environment of government have created new tensions and challenges for senior civil servants – especially in their relationship with ministers. In short there is 'trouble at the top'.

Our argument

The argument of this report, in essence, is that, while the civil service remains one of the best in the world on many measures, it suffers from a number of weaknesses. It is, of course, hard to make generalisations about an institution as complex and varied as Whitehall. But, our research (above all the evidence emerging from our interviews) suggests that, while civil servants are often dedicated, impartial and talented, Whitehall is poor at reflecting on its purpose, strategic thinking, dealing with inadequate performance, managing change effectively, learning from mistakes or working across departments. Corporate leadership is lacking.

Despite the drives over recent decades to recruit a wider range of specialists into the service and improve training within it, amateurism still too often prevails, reflecting a skills gene pool that is too narrow – management and delivery expertise, in particular, are still lacking. Though Whitehall has 'opened up' in recent years, the degree of mobility in and out remains limited, with many outsiders complaining of the difficulty they have in penetrating the core of the civil service. Civil servants tend to look upwards, rather than outwards, in a culture that still values proximity to ministers above all else. The focus upwards also means that the civil service often lacks an understanding of the public it serves.

We acknowledge that we are not the first to have levelled many of these criticisms. Most of the shortcomings we point to are of a long-standing nature and they have been the subject of many articles and publications over the years (for example, Balogh (1959), Fabian Society (1967), Barnett (1986), Ponting (1986), Bichard (2004; 2005), Straw (2004) and Darwell (2006)), as well as of official reports and associated reform efforts (including the Fulton Report (1968), Next Steps (1988), Continuity and Change (1994), Modernising Government (1999), and Delivery and Values (2003)).

We contend, however, that past reforms have not got to the root of the problem. Whitehall's weaknesses flow from the way it is *governed* – from the constitutional conventions that dictate who is responsible for what, who gets appointed to run the top echelons of the service and how, and what they are expected, allowed or encouraged to do. Yet, as we suggest in Chapter 5, past efforts to reform Whitehall have treated Whitehall's governance arrangements as sacrosanct, and instead focused on what are, according to our analysis, 'second order' matters.

The governance arrangements of an institution, we argue, play a vital role in shaping its culture, its sense of purpose, its capacities and capabilities – in short, its effectiveness. And Whitehall is no exception. Its governing conventions foster the culture, incentives and outlook of the service, shape and regulate the pivotal relationship between ministers and mandarins, and ultimately determine how and why the civil service behaves as it does. Yet the conventions governing Whitehall are seriously inadequate and out of date. In particular, we argue that the central convention of ministerial responsibility, while once, perhaps, effective, needs recasting. As it works now, the respective responsibilities of ministers and civil servants are unclear and lines of accountability confused.

Some might suggest that they did not need this report to tell them that civil service governance is a live issue. Hardly a week goes by without some news item raising questions about the 'politicisation of the civil service' and government assaults on its traditions of integrity and impartiality. But, our argument is that the debate about politicisation – a debate that is by no means new – is something of a diversion.[3] Were special advisers or other political appointees – the main agents of politicisation – to be abolished tomorrow, the basic problems with the way the civil service is governed would still exist. Rather than see politicisation as the core problem or key solution facing Whitehall, we understand it as a response, perhaps short-sighted, to the fundamental shortcoming in the way Whitehall is governed.

The governance vacuum

What, then, is precisely wrong with the way Whitehall is governed? This is best put by saying that lines of accountability are weak and confused. There is a 'governance vacuum' at the heart of Whitehall.

It is surprisingly hard to find an official characterisation of existing governance arrangements – roles and responsibilities remain largely uncodified. Nevertheless, a number of doctrines and conventions laid down in the 19th century are key.

The most important of these, ministerial responsibility, dictates that civil servants are accountable to ministers for their actions, and ministers are, in turn, accountable to Parliament. According to this doctrine, civil servants exist to assist ministers in advising on and executing government policy. But, ministers, and ministers alone, are answerable to Parliament, and ultimately to the electorate, for both the policies they instruct the civil service to execute and for their execution or 'operationalisation'. Indeed, a second, related convention – that of the 'anonymity' of civil servants – denies Parliament, or any other public body, the opportunity to interrogate civil servants or otherwise hold them to account in a meaningful way. As Turpin writes: the 'ancillary to ministerial accountability is the non-accountability of civil servants' (Turpin 1994).

If the convention of ministerial responsibility appears to give ministers power and responsibility over the civil service, others severely limit their space for manoeuvre. Jealously guarded conventions of recruitment and promotion by merit, 'permanence' and 'impartiality' prevent ministers from appointing, promoting, sanctioning or dismissing their staff, seeking independent advice, or forcing change on an unwilling service. Indeed, these conventions underpin an understanding of the civil service – still very powerful in Whitehall – as an autonomous profession, accountable to no one but itself.

These arrangements, which evolved throughout the mid 19th century, might have worked well in their early days, when government was small, Whitehall departments still smaller, and the job of managing both relatively simple. But they work less well now. Indeed, our contention is that they have become a recipe for ambiguity, confusion, weak leadership and buck-passing. Civil servants' and ministers' prerogatives and responsibilities are ill-defined, and relations between them inadequately regulated or managed. We suggest, indeed, that the tensions induced by Whitehall's 'governance vacuum' are becoming more pressing by the day, with mandarins and ministers recognising that roles and responsibilities urgently need recasting

– a view most recently acknowledged by ministers and officials in the Home Office, following a fundamental review of the department (Home Office 2006).

We will return to explore the problems with the civil service's governance arrangements and the constitutional conventions that underpin them in greater detail in Chapter 4, but as our claims in this area form the lynchpin around which the rest of our arguments revolve, we here lay out what we think are the main problems in more detail:

Lack of civil service accountability

- *External accountability:* The doctrine of ministerial responsibility means that civil servants are not subject to *external* or direct accountability for the roles and functions they perform. (The exception is that Permanent Secretaries are directly accountable to Parliament, through the Public Accounts Committee, for financial probity.) Parliament – and the outside world – have very limited powers to interrogate or scrutinise civil servants.

- *Internal accountability:* Ministerial responsibility rests on the understanding that civil servants are accountable to ministers, who are directly and exclusively accountable to Parliament. In fact, ministers cannot effectively hold civil servants to account. To do so would violate the conventions around recruitment and promotion on merit, and civil service impartiality. Ministers have very limited powers to choose their civil servants, promote them or dismiss them – or to seek redress when they feel that they are being poorly served. Consequently, *internal* accountability is weak.

Lack of ministerial accountability

- The ambiguities in the civil service's governing conventions mean that ministers are also insufficiently accountable for their performance. Despite the conventions supposedly guarding civil service independence, and protecting civil servants' right to 'speak truth unto power', civil servants are not in a good position to resist improper demands, challenge ministerial amateurism or prejudice, or object to the hiring or conduct of special advisers and other political appointees. The convention of ministerial responsibility dictates that civil servants exist to 'serve the government of the day', and that, by and large, means doing as ministers wish. If ministers insist on pursuing poorly worked out or attention-grabbing policies, so be it. It is the job of civil servants to support ministers in everything they do. And, when criticised by ministers, civil servants have very little opportunity to defend themselves. Civil servants, the theory goes, work directly for ministers, and have no 'constitutional personality' of their own.

Lack of clarity in Cabinet Secretary–Permanent Secretary relations

- Relations between Permanent Secretaries (the heads of departments) and the Cabinet Secretary (nominally the head of the civil service) are ill-defined. Permanent Secretaries are said to answer to their ministers, and, in their role as accounting officers, to Parliament. At the same time, the centre, in the form of Cabinet Secretary, Prime Minister and Treasury, make increasing demands on them, and exercise a growing, if mainly informal, authority over them. Too often, responsibility and accountability falls between the gaps in this arrangement.

It is our contention that these shortcomings in the governance arrangements at the top of the civil service have serious negative effects on civil service performance overall. Among other consequences, they:

- lead to an absence of clear corporate leadership, so detracting from the service's ability to think and act strategically or drive change.
- ensure that civil servants have a weak sense of individual responsibility; there is no tradition of feeling accountable for outcomes – too often there is no price for failure in Whitehall.
- militate against root and branch change – as a self-governing institution the civil service can, and in the past always has, avoided fundamental reform; there is no external pressure to change.
- allow ministers and civil servants to duck and dive behind one another when things go wrong.
- encourage civil servants to focus upwards on ministers, rather than outwards on civil society organisations and citizens.
- result in a neglect of managerial and operational matters – the doctrine of ministerial responsibility dictates that ministers are responsible not only for developing and applying policies, but for the strategic management and operations of their departments; yet, most ministers have little interest and even less capacity in issues of strategic management and operations.
- promote ministerial overload by drawing ministers into operational details.

Put more positively, we argue that a clear accountability system – one that clearly identifies the responsibilities of ministers and civil servants and ensures that they are held to account in executing these responsibilities – will force a step change in the civil service as a whole. With improved governance arrangements in place, the civil service will be able to be relied upon to 'innovate from within' (Leadbeater 2002).

Our recommendations

But how should relations between ministers and mandarins be divided up, and to whom should they be accountable? We end our report with some brief recommendations. We argue against one possible reaction to the problems that we have identified – greater politicisation of Whitehall. This, we argue, would result in a further transfer of power to Britain's already mighty executive, and might further discourage the civil service from looking outwards and engaging with citizens, local agencies and civil society.

Instead, we favour measures that would preserve the civil service's traditions of neutrality and objectivity, but ensure that civil servants – and ministers – are properly held to account for their performance. To this end, we argue that the convention of ministerial responsibility should be revised, so that, while ministers remain accountable for policy, resources and strategic decisions – including decisions about the role and structure of the civil service – civil servants become externally accountable for clearly defined operational matters.

Revising the doctrine of ministerial responsibility will only prove productive, however, if we can find ways of adequately supporting ministers and civil servants in their new roles and ensuring that they really are held to account for the way they handle their new responsibilities. This demands, in our view, a radical overhaul in the way the civil service is governed. Among other reforms, we recommend:

- The creation of a stronger, more centralised civil service executive, led by a civil service 'Head'. The Head of the Civil Service would, in consultation with the Prime Minister and individual ministers, appoint and line-manage Permanent Secretaries. He or she would have the power to reward high performers and remove under-performers. He or she would also be responsible for strategic management of core corporate functions and services, like human resources, knowledge management, information and communication technology, and financial management. Ministers, of course, would not only retain control over resources, they would have a power of veto over senior appointments and would be actively involved in informing the performance assessment of Permanent Secretaries. And they would, most importantly, remain responsible for setting policy.
- The establishment of a new governing body for the civil service. Appointed by Parliament, this would be responsible for setting the strategic direction for the service, appointing a civil service head, scrutinising performance, and laying out what is expected of civil servants and ministers and, where necessary, managing disagreements between them.
- The enhancement of Parliament's powers to hold ministers to account, and the creation of new powers to do the same for civil servants.

- The introduction of external performance assessment for all Whitehall departments.
- The creation of a Department for the Prime Minister and Cabinet, with the Cabinet Secretary becoming, in effect, the Permanent Secretary of the new department. This department would be responsible for running the Prime Minister's Office and serving the Cabinet and cabinet committees.
- The enshrinement of these reforms in a new Civil Service Act. The traditional doctrine of ministerial responsibility, though vague and contested, remains powerful, and it will be very difficult to establish new and clearer lines of accountability, unless ministerial responsibility is reformulated in statute.

A number of caveats: first, we willingly acknowledge that Whitehall has very real strengths. International surveys show that the British civil service remains one of the most admired in the world (Kaufman *et al* 2005). Competition for entry into the civil service is intense, ensuring that recruits are exceptionally able and qualified: the civil service came first in the Top 100 Graduate Employers Survey conducted for *The Times* in 2003, and second in 2004 and 2005 (*The Times* 2003, 2004, 2005). Training and support for senior civil servants is now much stronger than it was, and Whitehall is now much more open to outsiders. Objectives are more clearly defined than they were and most officials say they understand their goals. Old and invaluable traditions of hard work, public-mindedness and integrity are alive and well. Moreover, the weaknesses that remain are weaknesses not of individuals but of culture, system and, ultimately, governance.

Second, disagreements over the future of the civil service are often depicted as pitting advocates of increased politicisation against those loyal to the traditional values of anonymity, permanence and impartiality – or, more emotively, as pitting ministers against civil servants. We don't argue that the debate does sometimes take this form. But our report cannot be fitted into this framework.

We maintain that the existing arrangements serve both mandarins and ministers poorly. A clearer articulation of the prerogatives and responsibilities of civil servants and ministers, and more rigorous scrutiny of both will benefit all. Ministers will get a more effective civil service – and be in a position to focus on making policy. Civil servants will get greater freedom and greater responsibility for delivering on government objectives. In fact, we think, were there better governance arrangements, 'politicisation' would become less of an issue. Ministers are less likely to feel driven to make political appointments to drive change and improve standards. Civil servants will be less inclined to view political appointments as a threat.

Report structure

This report is structured in the following way. In Chapter 2 we reflect on the aims and roles of the civil service, and explore the bearing that recent societal changes have on these. We suggest that it is only if we understand how demands on Whitehall are changing that we can adequately understand how service itself needs to change. Chapter 3 draws on our research – especially our interviews – to lay out ways in which we believe the civil service is not performing as well as it could. Chapter 4 turns to explore further the failings in Whitehall's governance arrangements, and the links between these and weaknesses identified in Chapter 3. In Chapter 5 we make some broad-brush recommendations as to the direction of reform.

The civil service in a new century

There is no platonic archetype of a civil service. The form civil services take, and the job that they are expected to do, vary across time and place. At the same time, the role that a civil service should play at any one time is far from given or obvious. For these reasons, it is important, in an inquiry of this type, to begin by asking why we need a civil service, what the Whitehall civil service is for and for whom it exists to serve.

What we offer here, we should stress, is intended only as a sketch. The elaboration of a full account of the civil service's responsibilities should be led by the civil service itself. But some sense of its role is important if we are going get any purchase on the strengths and weaknesses of the existing civil service, or ways it needs to be reformed.

We note in passing that while all organisations find it hard to reflect on their purposes, Whitehall seems to find it harder than most. We argue that this is because of the weakness in governance arrangements already alluded to. No one is clearly responsible for reflecting on the strategic direction of the civil service. While most public and voluntary sector organisations are periodically obligated to articulate their values and identify their mission and goals, this is not true of the civil service. Whitehall, for example, lacks an equivalent to the BBC charter renewal process, which obliges the BBC to evaluate its role and justify its existence every decade. Instead, the civil service takes its role as given – to do what it has always done.[4]

What, then, is the role of the civil service? What purposes does it exist to serve?

One way of answering this question is simply to identify the jobs the civil service does – something we do in Box 2.1. This is a helpful exercise. For one thing, it should make us wary of overly simple comparisons with private sector organisations or reductive, one-dimensional understanding of what the civil service exists to do. It is not just a machine for implementing government policy, maximising public satisfaction, delivering public services, or even, on a slightly richer understanding, enabling people to help themselves. Put more positively, a list like this reminds us of the startling range of things for which the civil service is responsible – a range without comparison in any other institution, public or private. Try thinking of an organisation that is collectively responsible for indirectly managing health services, offering advice on matters as diverse as going to war, rewriting the Highway Code, designing and implementing a new strategy for childcare provision, collecting taxes, and issuing drivers' licences, to name but a few of its day-to-day tasks.

Box 2.1 The basic roles and functions of the Whitehall civil service

Policy advice to Ministers: Civil servants remain the primary source of policy advice for Ministers. They are responsible for:
- developing and designing policy
- managing the policymaking process
- preparing and drafting legislation.

Parliamentary and 'political': Civil servants, in supporting ministers, perform important 'housekeeping' duties. They:
- run ministerial offices
- steer ministers through political events
- manage the parliamentary process.

Management and delivery: Whitehall's responsibilities here include:
- Overseeing the strategic management of departments, ensuring they have the capabilities and capacity to deliver the government's objectives.
- The management of services that are directly delivered through their departments, for example, the immigration service.
- Arms-length management of those services delivered indirectly through their executive agencies – like the UK Passport Agency and the Child Support Agency – and Non Departmental Public Bodies (NDPBs).
- Indirect management of other public services like the NHS, and police and public corporations like the BBC.
- Whitehall also performs a crucial role in the regulation of the private and voluntary sectors.

Constitutional checks and balances: The civil service carries out important constitutional roles, though definitions vary and have been the source of much debate and interpretation.
- Upholding constitutional propriety, and making sure that ministers act within the parameters of the law.
- In their roles as accounting officers, Permanent Secretaries are also directly accountable to Parliament for the regularity, propriety and efficient use of public money spent by their departments.
- A less clearly defined role is that of 'speaking truth unto power'. Officials are expected to give free and frank advice to ministers, which will at times involve saying 'No, Minister'. The Civil Service Code states that 'Civil servants should conduct themselves with integrity, impartiality and honesty. They should give honest and impartial advice to the

cont. next page

> Minister ... without fear or favour, and make all information relevant to a decision available to them.' (Cabinet Office 1999)
> • Constitutional guardians – some have argued that the civil service is there to uphold and defend the 'public interest' (see Marquand 2004: 107).

This said, a list like this only takes us so far: for, it does not tell us much about the values the service should advance, the goals it should aim to achieve, the way it should be organised, or the new demands that are or will be made on it as society changes.

One way to address these questions is through a brief overview of the developments within the British civil service and the paradigms of public administration that have helped animate them. As we will see, the civil service passed through a number of distinct phases, each marked by a characteristic set of views about the needs the service exists to meet and the ways it should operate – views that are themselves based on profounder ideas about human nature, the good society and the role of the state.

This narrative will not, alas, lead us to a newly emerged paradigm, fit for the modern age. It is not at all clear that such a paradigm exists; the civil service is certainly not making use of it, if it does. But this historical overview will at least enable us to get a sense of the strengths and weaknesses of past frameworks, and offer us insights into the challenges the civil service faces today.

The modern British civil service is often said to have been the product of the famous Northcote-Trevelyan report of 1854. But it took more than half a century for Whitehall to develop into the sort of service advocated by Northcote-Trevelyan – that is, a permanent and unified service, based on the merit principles of appointment by open competition and promotion according to ability. By the 1930s, however, it approximated to what might be called the bureaucratic model of a democratic civil service – a model to which most other civil services in democracies of the same period also conformed (Northcote and Trevelyan 1854; Hennessy 2001; Bogdanor 2003; Stoker 2006).

This model had a number of distinctive traits. First, the civil service looked upwards, and all direction was provided from the top, by democratically elected leaders, ultimately accountable, through periodic elections, to voters. Second, the service itself was made up of full-time, lifelong professional administrators – civil servants – appointed and promoted on merit.

Relations within the service were also hierarchical, with goals for each layer of the service set by the layer directly above it. Great value was attached to the following of strict and defined procedures and rules – wherever possible, complex problems were broken down into manageable and competitive tasks, each the province of a particular office. Finally, bureaucratic civil services aimed to deliver fairly standardised services to the public. Many of these traits – hierarchical structure, division of labour, uniformity of provision – it shared, of course, with other large organisations of the period, like factories, armies, hospitals and schools.

The British variant of this model was distinctive in some ways. It had a strongly departmentalised character – civil servants answered ultimately to their minister, and, through him or her, to Cabinet and Parliament. The centre was always comparatively weak and under-developed. In comparison to some continental countries, notably France and Germany, or to British local government, the British civil service did not much prize professional training or expertise, believing instead in the gifted, classically trained generalist (Hennessy 2001).

'Character' – a word that played an important part in the Northcote-Trevelyan report – also played an important role in the British system, in maintaining standards of probity and public service, in resisting improper demands from ministers, tempering populism, and in ensuring that the 'machine' did not become too machine-like – that it preserved, as much as was desirable, flexibility and good judgement. Indeed, the self-understanding of Whitehall mandarins was shaped to no small degree by Platonic and Aristotelian ideals of gentlemanly good judgement, balance, and wisdom (Lind 2005). Finally, of course, and very much in keeping with the value attached to 'character', fundamental principles took the form of conventions rather than written codes.

It is important to acknowledge the achievements of the classical civil service. It is, as Vernon Bogdanor has written, 'a salutary corrective' to those who denigrate the so-called amateur civil service of the post-war years, to remember 'that it succeeded in establishing, under extraordinarily difficult conditions, The National Health Service, a new social security system, the expansion of education, and the nationalisation of major industries (Bogdanor 2001: 292). And, of course, important elements of it live on today (Stoker 2006). Indeed, some parts of the current civil service, having tried non-bureaucratic approaches, are reverting to older, more bureaucratic ones (Hood 2005). Modern government will always need bureaucracies.

In the 1970s and 1980s, however, civil services around the world, including the British civil service, were reformed according to a different model – that of New Public Management (NPM). In one respect, the old and the new models were alike. They both saw the civil service as an essentially apolitical thing – there to serve relatively simple goals that were identified from without. Important policy decisions were, on both models, to be made by the democratically accountable government of the day.

Nevertheless, the NPM model defined itself against the established bureaucratic model, as exemplified in Whitehall – a model that, it was argued, was fundamentally flawed and increasingly out of date. According to these criticisms, the traditional civil service, and other public agencies, suffered from 'producer capture'. Its departments were bloated and inefficient, and put the interests of those who worked for them above those of the public they were meant to serve. Rigid, over-unionised and self-serving, state bureaucracies patronised their 'clients' – they were disempowering. Services offered by the state compared unfavourably to services offered by the market.

New Public Management, then, aimed to introduce a 'bottom line' mentality to public services generally, and the civil service in particular. Efficiency became the key goal, as private sector models were fastened on to the machine of government (Osborne and Gaebler 1992). Wherever possible, services were privatised. Where this was not possible, other mechanisms were introduced – 'quasi-markets', purchaser provider splits, customer satisfaction surveys and other measurable performance indicators, audit and inspection regimes, and performance-related pay – aimed at producing market-type rigours. Clients were now described as 'customers', public sector professionals became 'service providers'.

Like the bureaucratic civil service of old, the NPM-inspired reforms have real achievements to their name – privatisation has often served the public well, as have the expansion of choice, responsiveness and accountability. Contemporary Job Centres, to take just one example, offer a much superior service to the dole offices and labour exchanges of old. Nevertheless, the model had serious shortcomings and has itself recently come into a great deal of criticism.

What, then, is wrong with the NPM approach to public administration? Critics complained that its attempts to recast the public sector on private sector principles risked undermining the public service ethos; that it cared about outputs – reduced costs, better services – at the expense of outcomes, did nothing to discourage the dumping of difficult problems on other agencies, and often created perverse incentives; that it was insufficiently sensitive to the variety of things government has to do. NPM sought to remodel the public sector on the private, but public institutions need to be guided by different criteria and meet different objectives from private ones.

Given the limitations to NPM approaches, it is not surprising that public management specialists and policymakers have been seeking different models of public administration and different principles to guide civil service reform – ones that incorporate insights from NPM thinking and build on its achievements, but also go beyond it. These specialists and policymakers inevitably disagree in details as to what alternative models might look like, but they tend to agree on a number of key points.

First, they insist on the need to recognise that government and its agencies exist to do much more than provide services, whether to 'clients' and 'users' (as on the classical public administration model), or 'customers' and 'consumers' (as on the NPM model). The efficient delivery of services is, of course, one of the main aims of government, but, beyond this, government is also properly concerned about a broader range of values and 'outcomes', as we have already suggested.

We look to government, for instance, to instil and maintain values of citizenship, equity and democracy, to change behaviour and, in some cases, reduce dependence on services, to care for the natural world, to create and perpetuate communities, even to build 'beauty', enrich culture, and further science. Many of these outcomes are arguably increasingly central to governments' tasks. It if often said, for instance, that government will never successfully tackle environmental problems, or problems of low-level crime and disorder, without changing values and behaviour (see ippr's forthcoming work on changing behaviour). New Public Management worked with an impoverished understanding of the public realm, taking the view that only things that can be counted count.

Moreover, in addition to concerning itself with delivering efficient services and effective outcomes, government needs to be in the business of developing support for its actions, winning buy-in and building legitimacy. On the older bureaucratic and NPM ways of thinking, legitimacy largely came from the formal democratic system – elected leaders set the priorities, and public agencies delivered on them.

Government, however, now takes place in very different circumstances: it is now in some ways weaker than it was and much more dependent on other actors, organisations and groups than was once the case. It has to work with a wider range of players – and these players do not always see it as the only legitimate actor. As a result, it has to be better at listening and co-operating. Below, we lay out some of the reasons why co-operation has become more important.

- As information has multiplied and expertise proliferated, so government's ability to solve problems for itself has declined – it needs to work closely with international organisations, independent experts, stakeholder groups and the like. Citizens, too – even, or perhaps especially, the least educated and most marginalised – hold knowledge about their needs and reactions, without which policy designed for them will fail.
- Public services are now frequently delivered not from the centre, but entail partnerships with private sector, not-for profit groups and independent or semi-independent public agencies. The 'ship of state', it has been said, 'has become a flotilla' (Peters 2001). Third, it is increasingly clear that many of the most intractable problems that government faces – especially problems of social exclusion – depend on multi-agency working, usually in the form of 'area-based initiatives'. Successful partnership working, or joined-up-government, has become something of a Holy Grail of modern governance.

- Many of the challenges that government now faces cannot be met even through the delivery of the most joined-up, or 'user-focused' services. They involve changing people's values and behaviour, enabling people to help themselves, building community capacity, 'social capital' and 'collective efficacy' or forging new relations of co-production. Government can't improve recycling rates, reduce crime, bring down unemployment, or manage increasingly common chronic conditions like diabetes or obesity, without engaging people as active partners or 'co-creators'. (The economy similarly works best where government listens to and works with business.)

- Government now has to work harder than it once did to earn and sustain legitimacy for its decisions. People are less deferential and, to some degree, less trusting of authority than they were. Special interest groups, campaigning bodies and the press now expect to be consulted and engaged. The same is true of ordinary people.

Finally, critics of NPM tend to argue that government needs to find less heavy-handed, more sophisticated ways of 'delivering' public services and encouraging public service improvement. Whitehall's attempts to micro-manage public service professionals, through an endless downpour of targets, directives, ring-fenced grants, inspections and audits, has, in particular, come in for a great deal of criticism, with critics like Onora O'Neill, Charles Leadbeater, David Marquand, Sue Goss and Jake Chapman calling for a new, more trusting, less hierarchical relation between those at the centre of government and those working with the public (O'Neill 2002; Leadbeater 2002; Marquand 2004; Goss 2005; Chapman 2002).

Clearly, all this has profound implications for the way government, public services, and the civil service in particular, have to work. The implications are sometimes expressed by saying that we need to move from government to networked *governance* (Karmarck 2003; Goldsmith and Eggers 2004; Stoker 2006). More practically, it means moving from a form of public administration and policymaking based on the principle that 'the gentleman in Whitehall knows best', in Douglas Jay's unforgettable formulation, to one where knowledge is recognised as widespread, and consultation, deliberation and consensus-building becomes central to everything government does (Jay 1947: 258). 'The pressure is on', as Gerry Stoker has put it, 'to find new ways to collaborate in an increasingly inter-dependent world' (Stoker 2006).

The significance of these changes can be exaggerated. Government has always needed to listen, to co-operate and to win support. Central government has always had to work with local government and others alternative source of power. And central and local government have always sought to engage with local people, not just as service users, but as citizens. Britain has long had a relatively vibrant civic culture (Almond and Verba 1989), at the same time, elected government quite properly continues, even in our more networked world, to retain a special authority. With its unique democratic mandate, it will always remain as more than just one among a number of 'stakeholders' or 'partners'; the public expects it to lead, regulate and arbitrate. Nevertheless, we increasingly look to government to produce a wide range of values, and to do so in a less hierarchical, more networked way. Officials need, as Goldsmith and Eggers have put it, 'to be more like symphony conductors than drill sergeants' (2004).

We have been gesturing to some of the goals we should expect a modern, 21st-century civil service to meet, and some of ways we might expect it to work. A number of public management experts, led by the Harvard thinker Michael Moore, have even sought to elaborate a new public management paradigm, a superior successor to the bureaucratic model and

---

Box 2.2 The civil service in a changing world

Whitehall does not exist in a vacuum. The demands on it change in response to developments in the wider environment. Today, Whitehall must reconcile itself with a number of long-term societal trends that are changing the context of government in the 21st century. These include:

- Globalisation and the realisation that many problems can only be solved through international co-operation
- Demographic change and the need to cope with an ageing and ever more diverse population
- Growing income inequality
- The information revolution
- Continued marketisation and the blurring of boundaries between public and private
- A less deferential and trusting citizenry
- Rising public expectations of government
- A more intrusive and pervasive mass media
- The increasing salience of 'wicked problems' – problems that require joined-up, networked approaches to tackle them
- Problems that can only be addressed through co-production and changing behaviour.

This list is far from comprehensive, but it demonstrates a crucial point. Societies are more complex and less governable than ever before. As Nye and Donahue (2003) argue, these trends are acting to 'diffuse a degree of power, responsibility and even legitimacy held by central government'.

Table 2.1 Three paradigms of public management

	Traditional public administration	New Public Management (NPM)	Public value management
Definition of the public interest	By politicians or experts; little in the way of public input	Aggregation of individual preferences, demonstrated by customer choice	Individual and public preferences produced through public deliberation
Key objectives	Politically provided inputs; services monitored through bureaucratic oversight	Managing inputs and outputs in a way that ensures economy and responsiveness to consumers	Overarching goal is achieving public value that in turn involves greater effectiveness in tackling the problems that the public most cares about; stretches from service delivery to system maintenance
Role of public managers	Clerks: To ensure that rules and appropriate procedures are followed	Efficiency maximisers: To improve service delivery quality To help define and meet agreed performance targets	Explorers: To steer networks of deliberation and delivery and maintain overall capacity of the system To respond to citizen/user mandate and trust through guaranteeing quality services
Role of policymakers	Commanders	Commissioners	Leaders and interpreters
Role of population	Clients (passive)	Customers (passive)	Co-producers and citizens (active)
Approach to public service ethos	Public sector has monopoly on service ethos, and all public bodies have it	Sceptical of public service ethos (leads to inefficiency and empire building) – favours customer service	No one sector has a monopoly on ethos; maintaining relationships between shared values is essential
Preferred system for service delivery	Hierarchical department or self-regulating profession	Private sector or tightly defined arms-length public agency	A range of alternatives, often with a preference for local over central delivery
Role for public participation	Limited to voting in elections and pressure on elected representatives	Limited	Crucial and multifaceted, engaging with customers, citizens and key stakeholders

cont. next page

Contribution to the democratic process	Delivers accountability: competition between elected leaders provides an overarching accountability	Delivers objectives: limited to setting objectives and checking performance, leaving managers to determine means	Delivers dialogue: integral to all that is undertaken, a rolling and continuous process of democratic exchange is essential

Source: adapted from Kelly and Muers (2002); Hartley (2005); Stoker (2006)

NPM – the so-called 'public value' model (see Moore 1995; Kelly and Muers 2004; Stoker 2006).

The public value model argues, along lines outlined above, for the differences between private and public organisations. It maintains that those charged with managing public organisations need to be concerned not just with providing efficient services to customers, but with advancing a broad and sometimes conflicting set of goals of the sort we have already identified. It characteristically takes a pragmatic stand as to whether services are best delivered through the public, private or voluntary sector, but it insists that public agencies need to engage with the public not just as customers, but as citizens who have rights and responsibilities towards the state.

We do not, in this report, claim that the British civil service should adopt a public value framework. While some organisations, including the BBC, the Arts Council England, and the Heritage Lottery Fund, have sought or are seeking to adapt public value thinking to their purposes, it is not clear to us that it is, at this stage at least, sufficiently developed or determinate to serve as a helpful guide to reform. Anyway, it is not our purpose to urge civil service to adopt this or that outlook, or operate according to one set of principles or another. The civil service needs to lead the debate about its future direction itself.

Our concern, instead, has been to suggest that, whatever framework or strategy the civil service develops, it will have to recognise that it, like all public agencies, exists in changed times and has to meet changed demands. It needs, in particular, to become a more outward-looking organisation, winning co-operation and buy-in from an increasingly wide array of parties, in order to deliver efficient public services, but also to achieve a broader range of outcomes.

We give the final word to one of our interviewees:

We lack a 21st century vision for the civil service ... one that understands its role in a modern and vibrant democracy. We need to redefine the role of the civil service as part of a wider effort to address the democratic malaise affecting Britain. But we never think about the civil service in such terms. It's time we did and the first thing this involves is moving beyond the narrow constitutional definition which sees no role outside serving ministers. We need to recast the relationship between the civil service, ministers and the public. (Former senior official)

3 Appraising Whitehall: strengths and weaknesses

This chapter offers an initial evaluation of civil service performance, focusing, in particular, on areas where Whitehall appears to be weak or underperforming. Our exposition draws mainly on our interview data and from material we have obtained from the civil service itself, but also from secondary sources.

Any attempt to appraise something as large and complex as the Whitehall civil service is bound to have its limits. Whitehall covers varied terrain, with each department seeming to operate within its own microclimate, and even within departments there are differences that only get detected following more-forensic inspection. A sweeping overview like ours, moreover, also has to contend with a terrain that is constantly changing.

Like so many other organisations today, Whitehall seems to have embarked on a course of almost permanent reform. Since landing the top job, the new Cabinet Secretary, Sir Gus O'Donnell – who promised on his first day to 'accelerate the pace of reform' – has launched a wave of initiatives. These include the Departmental Capability Reviews, a 10-Point Plan for Diversity, a new Civil Service Code, and the creation of a new Permanent Secretaries' Management Group. These reforms follow a series made by his predecessor, Sir Andrew Turnbull, which included the Professional Skills for Government programme and the establishment of a new National School for Government (see www.civilservice.gov.uk).

That said, we contend that it is possible to make certain Whitehall-wide generalisations, and that, while the civil service has changed profoundly in many ways over recent decades, and even over recent years, certain key traits persist. A surprisingly strong consensus has emerged from our interviews: on the whole, those working within the civil service tended to agree with those who had left it, who work with it, or simply observe it in action. Moreover, we believe that what we have found chimes with what others have found over the years, and what is evident in other research and studies, including those produced by the civil service itself.

This is an *initial* evaluation. We revisit some of this terrain in Chapter 4, in the belief that the analysis of the inadequacies in the way the service is governed that we offer in that chapter allows us a fuller understanding of the source and character of the service's other limitations.

What have we found? In essence, that, despite some heroic efforts to improve things, there is still much cause for concern. That's not to deny Whitehall's obvious talents – it is still highly regarded for its public service ethic, its ability to perform in a crisis, its political nose and, above all, for its intellectual capacity; this is something the Prime Minister has been keen to highlight: In his speech on civil service reform, he stated that 'there is an intellectual ingenuity in parts of the service that is remarkable in and rare in any field' (Blair 2004).

Nor is it to deny that parts of the service are excellent by any standards: the Department for International Development (DfID), HM Treasury, the Delivery Unit and the Strategy Unit were each singled out by several of our interviewees for praise.

Nevertheless, Whitehall is perceived by many, both within and outside, to be performing below par, and is considered hindered by a range of weaknesses that detract from its effectiveness in key areas, including policy design, project management and delivery, partnership working, public engagement, line management and leadership. The senior civil service's weaknesses look particularly worrying when set against the demands that we suggested, in the last chapter, any 21st-century civil service will have to meet.[5]

In the sections that follow, we offer a thematic appraisal of Whitehall's strength and weaknesses. Needless to say, the headings we employ are somewhat artificial: many of the qualities and weaknesses we discuss are inter-related.

- Skills and capabilities
- Strategy and policy
- Institutional memory
- Leadership and co-ordination
- Performance accountability

Skills and capabilities

As we have seen in the last chapter, the British civil service long tended to value gifted 'generalists' over trained 'specialists'. The unified civil service of the mid 20th century, staffed by Oxbridge-trained humanists, taken on in youth and kept on for life, was intended to ensure a healthy supply of them. Generalists certainly have their merits: they tend to take a broad view of matters, can be better at thinking innovatively and strategically and can better resist intellectual fads and fashions.

But, if organisations need generalists, they also need specialists – experts in financial management, human resources, project management, technology and so forth – and ever since the Fulton report of the mid 1960s, if not before, it's been widely agreed that the British civil service did not have enough of them. Critics contrasted the civil service's reliance on amateurs with the place that local government accorded to professionals, with most local authority departments being run by one class of professionals or another – lawyers, architects, civil engineers, accountants. Of course, over-reliance on professionals can bring its own problems (Bichard 2006).

The complaint that the civil service relied too heavily on gifted amateurs was closely related to another long-standing criticism: that Whitehall was too insular and civil servants drawn from too narrow a background and exposed to too limited a range of experiences. The overwhelming majority of appointments in the 20th-century civil service were made from within the ranks of the service itself – outsiders, even those who had proved themselves gifted administrators and innovators, had little chance of getting through the door. At the same time, career civil servants had little opportunity to work outside the service and learn how things were done elsewhere.[6] As Hayden Phillips has written, recalling the civil service of the late 1960s: 'Interchange with the private sector or the wider public sector was extremely rare'. Phillips recalls suggesting to his division head that he should visit a police force to discuss one of his projects. His reply: 'I wouldn't do that if I were you. It will prevent you from being properly detached' (Phillips 2005: 48).

These two weaknesses – amateurism and insularity – were finally related to a third. The background of the civil servants and the ethos of the service gave it a distinctly gentlemanly cast – it tended to value probity, tradition and respect for seniority over efficiency, effectiveness and innovation. The British Civil service was not the sort of place to which you applied if you were set on getting your hands dirty.

Box 3.1 The culture of Whitehall

The Whitehall of the inter- and post-war years had a famously distinct culture. Indeed, the civil service in its mid 20th-century heyday was not just a civil service, it was a way of life, with its own peculiar processes of recruitment and rites of initiation, and a distinctive hierarchy, dress code, ethos and argot. To be a member of the British civil service was like being a doctor or lawyer, architect or army officer – it gave you a prestigious identity and made you a member of carefully regulated and exclusive club. But the Whitehall club, smaller, and largely concentrated in the centre of London, was arguably the most selective and tightly bonded of all professional clubs.

Of course, the reforms of the last three or four decades, aimed at opening up Whitehall and increasing its professionalism, have inevitably changed and, to some degree, diluted its once formidable *esprit de corps*. Yet, many recent critiques of the civil service continue to complain of its insular and conservative mindset (see Leadbeater 2002; Straw 2004; Bichard 2005; Darwell 2006; while Marsh *et al* (2001) describe the senior civil service as an intensely 'culture-bound' organisation).

cont. next page

We heard similar complaints from some of those we interviewed.

The single biggest challenge in Whitehall is getting things done! It is great in emergencies but on the day-to-day stuff it is amazing what tactics you have to resort to, to get things done, especially if you want to take on conventional thinking. There is an inherent and institutional resistance to serious change. You have to find a coalition of the willing at the top, and often go outside the formal decision-making process. But doing all this is very time consuming. (Senior official)

Is there a culture of ambition in Whitehall? I think this is the central issue for us and the jury is still out. (Permanent Secretary)

It still feels like a club. (Ex senior official)

Whitehall has, of course, made large changes in response to these criticisms. These include drives to recruit a more varied range of staff, upgrade training, improve progression for those with specialist skills, encourage those from outside the service to join temporarily or permanently, make greater use of consultants, and promote secondment opportunities for its staff. For example, many of the recently launched reform initiatives are intended to deal with these problems: the Professional Skills for Government programme is designed to do away with the distinction between 'amateurs' and 'specialists', while the new National School for Government is intended to build the skills-base of the service.

Furthermore, there is no doubt that these reforms have done much to improve the civil service. The question is: have they improved it enough? Our research suggests room for doubt. Certainly those inside and especially outside the civil service continue to complain about the survival into the 21st century of traditional outlooks, working practices and values and, in particular, of a failure to value specialist expertise. Ministers in particular complained about the lack of specialist skills:

I am regularly frustrated by the lack of expertise in the department. People complain that we spend too much on outside consultants and others, but often we don't have a choice. (Minister)

There is no culture of thinking about specific skills – there is still a whiff of the amateur ... I've never heard of [Professional Skills for Government] – and have certainly not seen any evidence of it. (Minister)

The career structure is completely wrong in what it values and rewards. There are still countless numbers of senior civil servants who are responsible for managing large and complex organisations who have never run anything before. (Minister)

People who take this line of argument have plenty of ammunition at their disposal. A report into the fiasco over the Scottish Parliament building – which went ten times over its original budget – blamed the problems, at least in part, on a significant lack of project management expertise within the civil service (Fraser 2004).

Earlier in 2006, the National Audit Office published a highly critical report of the Home Office for its failure to deliver its accounts to the Comptroller and Auditor General, Sir John Bourn, by the statutory deadline. It detected major errors and failures in the way senior management put them together. Bourn said: 'The pervasive and fundamental nature of the problems encountered in my audit of the Home Office's accounts for 2004-05 mean that I am unable to reach an opinion as to whether they show a true or fair view' and that the problems 'reflected a lack of skills within the accounts branch compounded by late recognition by management of the serious problems being encountered' (National Audit Office 2006). Outsiders were astonished to learn that the Home Office, which spends over £13 billion of public money a year, did not have a qualified professional finance officer sitting on its senior management board. Indeed, it was not until April 2005 that the Home Office appointed a professionally qualified Director General of Finance (National Audit Office 2006). One Permanent Secretary admitted that 'it is extraordinary that in 2005 we still don't have professional finance directors in place on all departmental boards'.

Finally, an internal report into the effectiveness of the Foreign and Commonwealth Office (FCO) that found its way into the public domain in August 2005 painted a bleak picture of organisational incompetence: 'Employees are seen as generalists so that a lack of professional competence or experience in, say, finance or human resources … is accepted even where it acts as a significant drag on the effectiveness of a department.' The report blamed weak management skills and a culture averse to change, the result of which was that:

> … people are frustrated and impeded in the execution of critical tasks by the weakness of the organisation, yet are unwilling to tackle the root causes that are entrenched in, and reinforced by the established culture. The entire organisation needs to be challenged and reformed, but the leadership lacks the skills needed and the will to upset the status quo. (*The Guardian*, 4 August 2005)

These are, admittedly, only a few examples drawn from an enormous organisation that manages much of our public life. Critics, the civil service's defenders will say, only notice when things go wrong, not the many times when they go right. But the critics' case does not just rest on anecdote and assertion.

An expert civil service?

It is interesting to note, for instance, that, as the civil service's own information shows, those with operational or other expertise are still far outnumbered by those who do not. In a staff survey of the senior civil service (SCS) in 2004, respondents were asked which area (from the recently launched Professional Skills for Government Programme) they would say closely fits the *majority* of their experience – policymaking, operational delivery or corporate services. The results showed that around 60 per cent of senior civil servants have a policy background compared to 25 per cent with most experience in service delivery and just 17 per cent with a background in corporate services (adapted from Cabinet Office 2005).[7] The senior civil service, it seems, has still not lost all its bias against management and operational delivery (see Talbot 2004). Moreover, as Table 3.1 shows, while some departments have a relatively large proportion of staff with a background in operations or corporate services, others do much worse. So, while a third of those in the Home Office and 27 per cent in Department of Health have primarily operational experience, this is true of only 19 per cent of those in the Department for Education and Skills and only 16 per cent in what was the Office of the Deputy Prime Minister – now the Department for Communities and Local Government.

Table 3.2, showing the percentage of senior civil servants who hold professional qualifications, offers another take on the extent to which the civil service is breaking out of its old generalist mould. Even acknowledging the rise in those who hold professional qualification between 2002 and 2004, it is still a major concern that just 36 per cent of the SCS have a professional qualification.

More worrying still, civil service expertise tends to be concentrated in important but, nevertheless, traditional areas like accountancy and the law. Expertise in more modern areas, like project management, communications and marketing, human resources, financial management, organisational behaviour and ICT, is often lacking. For instance, just two per cent of the SCS claimed to have a professional qualification in human resources (HR) as of 1 April 2004 (Cabinet Office/ippr).

Perhaps Whitehall's limited skills set (especially the lack of corporate service skills like procurement and financial management) and the persistence of generalism help explain why only a third of the senior civil servants believe that their organisation 'manages change effectively' (see Figure 3.1).

Table 3.1 Senior civil service skills groupings, by department

Department	Corporate services e.g. finance, human resources, procurement %	Policy (incl. arms-length delivery) %	Operational delivery e.g. service delivery %
SCS overall	17	59	25
Cabinet Office	18	51	31
Department for Constitutional Affairs	27	41	31
Department for Culture, Media and Sport	6	81	13
Department for Education and Skills	13	68	19
Department for Environment, Food and Rural Affairs	15	62	23
Department for International Development	4	65	32
Department for Trade and Industry	11	68	22
Department for Transport	14	52	34
Department for Work and Pensions	34	41	26
Department of Health	12	61	27
Foreign and Commonwealth Office	11	72	16
HM Treasury	15	84	1
Home Office	10	57	33
Ministry of Defence	34	35	31
Northern Ireland Office	22	43	35
Office of the Deputy Prime Minister	13	71	16

Source: adapted from Cabinet Office/ippr

Note: totals across rows may not sum to 100 per cent due to rounding

Table 3.2 Percentage of senior civil service that holds professional qualifications

Year	Percentage
2002	28
2003	31
2004	36

Source: Cabinet Office/ippr

Note: the great majority of these are made up of mainly traditional 'specialist' professions: lawyers, engineers, accountants, medical professionals and teachers

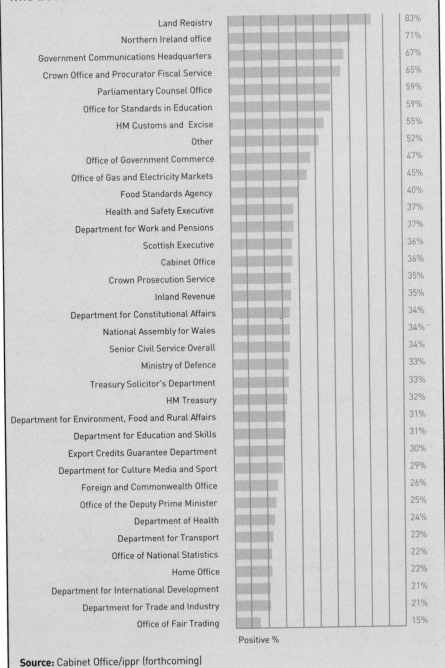

Figure 3.1 Number and percentage of senior civil service members who believe civil service leaders manage change effectively

	Positive %
Land Registry	83%
Northern Ireland office	71%
Government Communications Headquarters	67%
Crown Office and Procurator Fiscal Service	65%
Parliamentary Counsel Office	59%
Office for Standards in Education	59%
HM Customs and Excise	55%
Other	52%
Office of Government Commerce	47%
Office of Gas and Electricity Markets	45%
Food Standards Agency	40%
Health and Safety Executive	37%
Department for Work and Pensions	37%
Scottish Executive	36%
Cabinet Office	36%
Crown Prosecution Service	35%
Inland Revenue	35%
Department for Constitutional Affairs	34%
National Assembly for Wales	34%
Senior Civil Service Overall	34%
Ministry of Defence	33%
Treasury Solicitor's Department	33%
HM Treasury	32%
Department for Environment, Food and Rural Affairs	31%
Department for Education and Skills	31%
Export Credits Guarantee Department	30%
Department for Culture Media and Sport	29%
Foreign and Commonwealth Office	26%
Office of the Deputy Prime Minister	25%
Department of Health	24%
Department for Transport	23%
Office of National Statistics	22%
Home Office	22%
Department for International Development	21%
Department for Trade and Industry	21%
Office of Fair Trading	15%

Source: Cabinet Office/ippr (forthcoming)

Partly to correct its skills deficit, and partly to tackle its cultural insularity, much civil service reform has been motivated by the need to make Whitehall more permeable to outsiders, and to enhance the level of inter-change between the civil service and other organisations.

Turning to Whitehall's recruitment of external experts first, it is clear that real progress has been made:

- In 2004, it is estimated that 'outsiders' made up almost 20 per cent of the SCS.
- In 2003/04, 42 per cent of SCS vacancies were opened up to external competition.
- During 2003/04, there were 528 new entrants to the SCS; 160 (30 per cent) came from outside.
- Nearly one in four of staff currently at board level (defined as Director-General level, the most senior official in a department) has been directly appointed from outside the service.

(Cabinet Office/ippr; Levitt and Solesbury 2005)

Indeed, some civil servants are concerned that the service might be taking on too many external experts:

Some departments have gone too far. The Department for Health [DH] is the best example, where the traditional mandarin is a species threatened with extinction. The danger here is that the DH runs the risk of almost perfect producer capture. We do need to guard against such excesses. (Permanent Secretary)

Others, however, thought the service as a whole was getting it about right:

Some think that we have gone too far with the number of outsiders. My own view is that we are quite close to where we want to be. There is a danger that if we go too far then we will lose our collective mem-ory and the public service ethos will suffer. (Permanent Secretary)

While strides have been made, however, issues remain. First, as Table 3.3 shows, the number of externally appointed civil servants varies greatly across departments. Over a third of SCS staff working in the Department of Health and the Cabinet Office joined the civil service from outside. But, in the DTI and MOD, outsiders make up less than 10 per cent of SCS staff, and in the Foreign and Commonwealth Office they comprise just two per cent (the FCO comes under 'other departments' in Table 3.3).

Second, few outsiders make it to the very top ranks of Whitehall. Here, the career civil servant – the 'lifer' – remains supreme.

It is still the case that most civil service leaders come from the tradi-tional mandarin ranks. Despite the great fanfare about the recent

Table 3.3 'Outsiders' in the senior civil service

Large grouped department	Members in post 2004	External members		External recruits as % of all members	
		2003	2004	2003	2004
Cabinet Office	177	157	66	41	37.3
Department for Culture, Media and Sport	27	29	3	5	11.1
Department for Education and Skills	125	123	31	26	24.8
Department for Environment, Food and Rural Affairs	186	182	20	13	10.8
Department for Trade and Industry	251	249	23	17	9.2
Department for Transport	145	124	22	12	15.2
Department for Work and Pensions	249	227	45	37	18.1
Department of Health	370	397	130	142	35.1
HM Customs and Excise	108	113	5	5	4.6
HM Treasury	100	85	12	9	12.0
Home Office	236	218	55	40	23.3
Inland Revenue	289	280	20	19	6.9
Ministry of Defence	249	263	21	22	8.4
Office of the Deputy Prime Minister	204	132	48	29	23.5
Other departments	969	911	178	148	18.4
Scottish Executive	208	210	48	46	23.1
Total	3893	3700	727	611	18.7

Source: Levitt and Solesbury (2004)

changes around the Permanent Secretary table, the truth is that almost all of them are traditional, though very able, civil servants who have made their reputation by getting on with ministers, and who have never really run anything themselves. (Permanent Secretary)

This claim is borne out by the figures: of the current 29 Permanent Secretaries, six have been directly recruited externally, and a Cabinet Secretary has never been recruited from outside.[8]

Finally, it appears that, while the SCS has got better at recruiting experts to it ranks, it is not so good at making them feel welcome – or even retaining them.

I remained an 'outsider' when working in Whitehall and found it very difficult to penetrate the civil service culture. I found that doors didn't open because of my outsider status. It was extremely frustrating.

As an outsider you noticed the hierarchy much better than the insiders do. It's still too closed and it still feels like a club. (Ex senior official)

Furthermore, this was acknowledged to be a problem even by some of the career civil servants we interviewed.

There is still too much a sense of two worlds: the insider and the outsider. These two worlds need to be more integrated. We don't want to see the joints as much as we do. (Permanent Secretary)

Many outsiders often seem destined to fail within the current set-up. (Senior official)

More particularly, several of our interviewees said the civil service was poor at inducting outsiders into the service or supporting them through their early years, with the results that outsiders often leave, feeling frustrated or unfulfilled.

There are still too many examples of outsiders being brought in and not used effectively. At its worst this can involve the civil service deliberately moving talented people into parts of the department where they have no expertise. Someone we brought in for their financial expertise found herself in the consumer affairs unit. How pointless is that? (Minister)

This is backed by a recent Economic and Social Research Council study into the experience of 'outsiders', which concluded that many find it very difficult to penetrate Whitehall's 'insider' culture: 'There were many examples of insider processes that our interviewees identified as barriers to progress' (Levitt and Solesbury 2005).

Insiders getting out: secondments

While Permanent Secretary at the Treasury, Sir Gus O'Donnell was fond of saying: 'if you want to get on, get out' (O'Donnell 2006). Movement outside the service is now meant to be encouraged. Yet, several of our interviewees suggested that the service record is mixed at best.

We have not gone far enough here. We need to get our own people out more. (Permanent Secretary)

The figures again bear this out. Survey data obtained from the Cabinet Office suggest that, in 2004, 23 per cent of the SCS 'had some secondment experience outside the civil service' (Cabinet Office/ippr). But the rate varies greatly across departments (see Table 3.4), with the big delivery departments that would arguably benefit from secondment most having some of the lowest rates – only nine per cent of senior civil servants working in the Home Office and twelve per cent in the DTI have been seconded to work outside Whitehall.

Moreover, several of our interviewees expressed doubts about whether the civil service had really embraced secondment. One spoke of the 'colonial visit mentality, where officials go and spend a day in Kent and come back thinking they've cracked local government.' Another suggested that government departments do very little in the terms of trying to learn from people's experience.

> There is no appraisal of secondments. No one asks: did it work? What have you learnt? And what can we learn from you? (Senior official)

Table 3.4 Senior civil service with secondment experience outside the civil service by department, as at 1 April 2004

Department	Percentage with secondment experience
Cabinet Office	19
Department for Constitutional Affairs	18
Department for Culture, Media and Sport	30
Department for Education and Skills	14
Department for Environment, Food and Rural Affairs	40
Department for International Development	27
Department for Trade and Industry	12
Department for Transport	26
Department for Work and Pensions	23
Department of Health	8
Foreign and Commonwealth Office	36
HM Customs and Excise	42
HM Treasury	54
Home Office	9
Inland Revenue	11
Ministry of Defence	46
Northern Ireland Office	46
Office for the Deputy Prime Minister	39
Total*	23

Source: Cabinet Office/ippr

*Note: this is the total figure for the whole SCS including all departments and agencies

Strategy and policy

> The most important contribution to better performance is better policy. (*Better Policy Delivery and Design,* Cabinet Office 2001)

Whitehall has always prided itself on its ability to offer strong analytical policy advice to its political masters – and this pride is generally felt to be justified. Most criticism of the civil service, from within and outside, has been directed at its ability to 'manage' or 'deliver' services and outcomes, rather than develop policy. Nevertheless, incoming governments have usually attempted to improve the civil service's policymaking capacity – Harold Wilson, for instance, established a policy unit in No. 10, and Ted Heath created the Central Policy Review Staff (CPRS).

New Labour has followed suit – indeed it has gone further than its predecessors. Arguing that Whitehall policymaking was still too unstrategic, unfocused and un-joined-up, the Blair government introduced a range of measures including:

- the setting up of a dedicated Strategy Unit in the Cabinet Office
- beefing up the No. 10 Policy Unit
- the creation of cross-cutting policy units such as the Social Exclusion Unit
- the creation of departmental strategy units
- the advent of Public Service Agreements and five-year departmental strategic plans
- the partial opening up of the policymaking process to external policy academics and stakeholders
- the use of policy reviews and commissions such as those initiated by HM Treasury, which are typically headed by expert outsiders working with Whitehall officials.

Taken together, these and related innovations represent a significant step forward. One sign of their success is that many of them have caught the attention of international observers who now regularly visit the UK, interested in emulating Whitehall innovations.

Furthermore, perhaps the most important development under New Labour is in the recognition that policy is itself a specialist discipline. For too long, it had been assumed that policymaking, as practised by the gifted amateur, was something that civil servants simply did. This is reflected in the Professional Skills for Government (PSG) programme, which has a dedicated 'policy' profession grouping.

Yet, the evidence from our interviews and elsewhere suggests that Whitehall has some way to go before it lives up to its reputation for policymaking excellence. Parts of the Whitehall machine have improved dramatically, but elsewhere progress has been much more patchy.

> The first thing I noticed when I got into Whitehall was just how inaccurate the Rolls Royce machine label was when it comes to policy. I was confronted by people who had very few specific skills and little understanding of evidence-based policymaking. (Ex senior official)

A number of themes emerged. First, many suggested that government is still not as strong as it needs to be at strategic thinking – for instance, examining long-term developments, exploring cross-cutting challenges or reviewing options for radical reform.[9]

As stated, several of our interviewees suggested that the Cabinet Office's Strategy Unit has made an important contribution to Whitehall's strategic capacity. The development of departmental strategy units was also welcomed, though it is perhaps too early to assess their effectiveness. But some of our interviewees saw the Strategy Unit and its departmental counterparts as having a slightly insecure basis in the senior civil service, and doubted whether the service or many ministers placed enough value on strategic thinking: '[Whitehall] still creates isolated pockets of long-term thinking among a government machine fixated on the next four years' (Goss 2005). Government barely manages to think years ahead, let alone decades ahead.

Many of ippr's interviewees also complained about the closed and hidebound nature of the civil service's policymaking processes and thinking (see also Foster 2005b), though this complaint took a variety of different forms:

- Some complained about the failure of Whitehall to look beyond itself – that too often policymaking is done behind closed doors, with little attempt to engage stakeholders or capitalise on outside expertise. Elsewhere, Sue Goss has written critically of an 'invisible hierarchy' that shapes the way that Whitehall views policy experts in the rest of the public sector and beyond, while Geoff Mulgan, a former head of policy at No. 10, has complained that the 'we know best' mentality remains pervasive – that the default position is to be closed and secretive (Goss 2005; Mulgan 2005a). Jake Chapman makes a similar point when he suggests that, in Whitehall, 'stakeholders' tends to mean other government departments (Chapman 2002). We heard the same arguments ourselves:

  > The approach to policymaking has a long way to go. It needs to be prised open, involving universities, the professions, academics and think tanks much more than it currently does. (Ex senior official)

  > Whatever Whitehall says about opening up, in many important respects it remains a closed shop. There is nowhere enough movement between the civil service and the public sector and, consequently, Whitehall remains uninformed about how to reform public services. (Senior public sector figure)

- Some argued that, despite the rhetoric, there is still too much of a gulf between those designing policy in Whitehall and those delivering it (see also Chapman 2002). Even departments' own agencies complain about a sense of disconnection, lamenting the fact that they are rarely asked to contribute their views on policy development (Office of Public Services Reform 2002). Not enough thought is given to how the Whitehall can be informed by experience from the frontline. Yet it is crucial that this happens and that new ways are developed to facilitate this; for example, the opportunities provided by modern technology have yet to be seized upon.

> A crucial challenge for the civil service (and ministers) is to think about how it can breakdown the barriers between themselves and the public sector, which is such a rich source of ideas, innovation and expertise. We need mechanisms by which we allow those delivering policy at the coal face to feed back their ideas to those designing policy. Someone working in a Jobcentre Plus should be involved in policy development. We cannot think of them simply as part of the delivery arm. (Minister)

- Some complained of Whitehall's weakness when it comes to public engagement – especially public engagement of a deliberative kind. There have been some exceptions – notably the Department of Health's use of deliberative techniques in developing its public health White Paper (Department of Health 2006). Yet, it has been local government and local public services that have tended to make most use of 'new democratic processes' and to do so most imaginatively (Clarke 2002).

> Whitehall has no conception – other than the minister – of who the customer is and what they want. It has got better at engaging with the public through consultation but where it is really weak is when it comes to understanding the population it serves. It has very poor market research capacities and consequently finds it hard to know what the public thinks. At a time when the population is becoming more complex and diverse in Britain, it is crucial that the civil service has a better capacity here. (Ex senior official)

> It is staggering to compare the way that Whitehall develops policy with how a modern company develops its products and goods. In Whitehall there is simply no focus on the consumer and on what they want. No 'market research' takes place. If we want to use public engagement techniques then we simply have to bring in outside expertise since the civil service lacks the capabilities. (Minister)

- Most complained about Whitehall's relative weakness when it comes to learning from others. True, the service is much less insular than it was 30 years ago. But interviewees were quite amazed, for instance, at how little effort the civil service put into synthesising and collating information on public sector or local government innovation. This was also highlighted in a 2003 Strategy Unit report *Innovation in the Public Sector* (Strategy Unit 2003a). Devolution offers another example: One of the key arguments for devolution was that it would create a series of 'policy laboratories' across the nations of the UK. Yet, Whitehall has developed no systematic processes for monitoring policy innovation in Scotland, Wales or Northern Ireland (Adams and Schmuecker 2005).

- Others spoke negatively about a Whitehall tendency to opt for the 'safety first' option – or, worse, to be captured by 'client groups' and professional interests.

> Parts of our department act as NGOs for particular groups and sectors. The emotional commitment some officials have to particular sectors is incredible. The only concern I have with outsiders is that they tend to have even more emotional attachment, as they very often come from those sectors. (Senior civil servant)

Some argued that the quality of policy advice is diluted by Whitehall's passion for compromise and consensus building – a criticism voiced by the Prime Minister himself (Blair 2004). 'Buy-in' is sought from every quarter.

> There is still a widespread lack of imagination. A constant frustration for the PM was that the centre always had to come up with 'all the radical ideas'. It seemed that the departments were not capable of radical thinking. Why is this? It is probably because of the endless engagement departments have with stakeholders. This can act as a real drag on innovation if you have to constantly get 'buy-in', and the net result is you end up with watered-down policy. The centre, on the other hand, does not have this problem. It is set aside from stakeholders and is not hemmed in by the lobby groups. (Ex senior official)

- Finally, a number of the experts we spoke to criticised the tendency for policy to be driven by ministerial or prime ministerial conviction or by short-term political expediency, rather than by informed and considered analysis of evidence and arguments. The decision to invade Iraq, or various education policies – the rolling out of city academies, the abandonment of Tomlinson's recommendations for A-level reform – were cited as examples. These criticisms tended to be directed at ministers first and foremost – though it was recognised that they in turn were responding to the media's demand for a continuing output of new stories. Yet many complained about the civil service's lack of ability or inclination to stand up to ministers or blow the whistle when policy-making falls below standard – to say 'No, Minister'. As Donald Savoie has put it: 'Civil servants have become reluctant to explain why things must be so, to provide objective, non-partisan advice, and to explain what kind of trade-offs are required if a certain decision is taken, and so on' (Savoie 2005: 35). One of our interviewees put it down to a lack of expertise:

> When it comes to speaking truth unto power, you find that it is the outsiders who are actually better at this since they tend to have the real expertise and professional weight to say 'hang on a minute, minister'. And ministers do tend to listen to this more than traditional civil servants. (Permanent Secretary)

Others argued that ministers would be more ready to defer to their civil servants and listen to their arguments if they had more faith in their policymaking capacity. Certainly the ministers and ex-ministers we interviewed expressed a very acute degree of dissatisfaction with Whitehall's policymaking capacity.

> If the civil service performed better – not just at delivery and implementation – but also when it comes to policy, then we would probably listen to them more when they challenge us. As it stands, ministers, have either lost confidence in the ability of the civil service or think that it deliberately wants to thwart our plans. There is too much suspicion at the moment. (Minister)

Whitehall's institutional memory

Every organisation of any complexity needs to find ways of ensuring that the knowledge and experience that it contains are effectively preserved and deployed (Straw 2004). Yet, many of our interviewees suggested that Whitehall often falls down in this regard – that its 'institutional memory' (to use the management jargon) is relatively weak.

This comes as a surprise. After all, it is meant to be one of the great advantages of the 'Whitehall' model of a 'permanent' civil service staffed by career officials that it ensures that the people at the top of the organisation – people who have spent their whole lives working in it – have between them a long 'memory'. They will, over many years of working for the same organisation, have learned the lessons of their successes and mistakes and transmitted that learning to others. But, it seems that Whitehall is growing forgetful in its old age.

There is no attempt in Whitehall to think about knowledge management. Indeed, it often seems as though the wrong things are remembered. The corporate memory as a whole is lacking and poor corporate memory means you will be bad at change and knowing what works and what doesn't. This is frustrating because it is relatively simply to do something about. (Ex senior official)

Our interviewees pointed to a number of illustrations to make their point. These included Whitehall's poor record when it comes to major IT projects and procurement more generally. Instead of learning from the expensive failures, the service seems merely to repeat them.

What explains Whitehall's poor institutional memory? We highlight three important factors: brevity of tenure, departmentalism and lack of a culture of evaluation and learning.[10]

Over the last 20 years, Whitehall has encouraged a high level of movement between posts with the aim of building up the skills base of its officials. Yet, the indications are that this drive has now been taken too far, undermining governmental performance in the process. Cabinet Office data reveals that, in 2004, the average time spent in post for a member of the SCS was 4.1 years, with the median figure being just 2.9 years (Cabinet Office/ippr). The SCS staff survey shows that only eight per cent of the SCS have been in post for more than five years (Cabinet Office 2005).

Anecdotal evidence, moreover, suggests that movement between posts is even greater at junior levels, with younger civil servants often spending no more than a year in post before moving on. One ex-official we spoke to referred to this as the 'shopping trolley' syndrome: officials seem to collect positions like trophies, with promotion going to the one with the greatest collection. A number of outsiders complained that it was unusual to attend two meetings on a subject and find the same civil servants at both. One cabinet minister joked to us that he was his department's 'institutional memory', as he has been in post longer than any of his senior officials.

Second, Whitehall's learning capacity is hampered by its strongly departmental structure. We say more about departmentalism and the problems it causes below. It is enough to say here that the tendency for departments to be run as semi-independent organisations means that that lessons learned within one are not always available to another facing a similar challenge. The trend, which set in during the 1980s, towards departmental 'disaggregation' – the division of departmental research teams, policy teams and delivery teams into separate units – has had a similar effect (Page and Jenkins 2005; Goss 2005).

Finally, despite its reputation for being over-wedded to process and the written word, Whitehall does not tend to map formally its expertise or record its knowledge. It lacks a learning culture. The civil service is particularly poor at considered evaluation of its successes and, above all, its failures. As many philosophers and public management thinkers have argued, failure is inevitable and organisations need to learn from it (Popper 1945; Chapman 2002; Seddon 2003). Yet, Whitehall tends to seek to cover up its failures rather than build on them. It is unusual, for instance, for the service to undertake a thorough evaluation of a project or initiative and make a record of this.

> The mantra of 'what matters is what works' is often undermined by the fact that we don't know what works, and, even when we know that something doesn't, we go ahead and do it anyway. (Senior official)

Leadership and co-ordination

Some of the most common criticisms made of Whitehall in the course of our interviews were addressed at what is seen to be its un-strategic, un-reflexive and poorly co-ordinated approach to its tasks. The lack of effective leadership was regularly highlighted.

> A major weakness with Whitehall is the way it is governed. No one leads the service. The role of the Cabinet Secretary is poorly defined here. (Ex senior official)

> Whitehall lacks real leaders – especially at the top. The mandarin class simply have no experience of driving organisational change. No other organisation would appoint the equivalent of a senior civil servant – in terms of skills and experience – to manage complex change. To do so would break all the rules of modern HR. (Ex senior official)

Many of our interviewees argued, in particular, that the position of the Cabinet Secretary, and his or her department – the Cabinet Office – were simply too weak to do the job needed of them:

> The Cabinet Secretary is constitutionally weak vis-à-vis departmental Permanent Secretaries. There is no Whitehall equivalent of the local authority chief executive, no one who drives the machine corporately, with a strong vision. (Senior official)

> The Cabinet Secretary has no real power or leverage over the departments. He is institutionally weak … and can only ever drive change if there is a palpable sense that the alternative will be worse (Ex senior adviser)

> There are problems with the position of the Cabinet Secretary. Historically, because of the constitutional position of Permanent Secretaries as accounting officers, and, because of their sacrosanct

relationship with ministers, the Cabinet Secretary has always been very cagey about adopting a 'line management' role. This is beginning to change, but it needs to be institutionalised in some way. (Permanent Secretary)

The roots of this state of affairs can be traced, at least in part, to Britain's tradition of cabinet government. Unlike presidential systems, which invest great formal powers in the head of the government, the British Prime Minister had relatively little formal control over the Whitehall departments. Authority rested with individual ministers, each with a department to match his or her portfolio. In the past, many departments – especially the big departments of state – operated almost as independent entities, with their own structures, processes and culture (Smith 1999). The Prime Minister was expected to govern through his ministers, or with their co-operation.

The Prime Minister's own relative weakness was naturally mirrored in that of his 'department', comprising 10 Downing Street and, latterly, the Cabinet Office, and also in the position of the Cabinet Secretary. The Prime Minister has, it is true, gained in power over the last half century – and the power of the Cabinet Office has increased accordingly (Foster 2005a). So, the Cabinet Office plays a leading role, along with the Treasury, in setting the strategic direction of Whitehall departments and evaluating performance. And the Cabinet Office has grown centres of expertise and co-ordination – the so-called 'alphabet units' – including the Strategy Unit, the Delivery Unit and the e-Government Unit. As of July 2006, the Cabinet Office was recorded as having 11 different units under its roof.

Nevertheless, much of the power the Prime Minister has gained is informal or personal in character. The Cabinet Secretary rather than executive chairman or chief executive is still, in standing and powers, very much first among equals (Foster 2005; ippr interviews). And the Cabinet Office remains a relatively small, low-profile 'rag bag' department that has been 'unkindly described as the rest home of the pet projects of past prime ministers' (Rhodes 2005: 5; see also Dynes and Walker 1995). It is certainly not considered an effective department for driving strategic reform across the civil service (Thomson 2006). Critics point to the unhelpful conflation of important corporate functions with the more traditional role of servicing the Cabinet.

This system had and has its merits. It militated against the centralist character of the British constitution, ensuring that, if the British government is an 'elected dictatorship', it is a least the dictatorship of a committee and not of one man. And it allowed departments, at least in theory, to experiment with different approaches and learn from one another.

That said, most of our interviewees argued that the departmentalised character of Whitehall was now seriously holding government back. We distinguish three problems in particular.

Weak reflective capacity

First, the lack of a strong strategic centre means that the civil service has, in the past, had only very limited powers of self-examination or self-direction. As we suggested in the last chapter, it is poor at reflecting on fundamental questions about its purpose, role, shape or size.[11] This lack of self-examination and direction means the civil service can 'sleepwalk' into new territory and assume new roles, without any clear sense of purpose. For example, in Whitehall and beyond it is widely said that Whitehall needs to be better at 'delivery' – and a series of related initiatives has been launched – but the delivery role of Whitehall has never been clearly articulated.

> The purpose of civil service reform is never really defined. Often it's reform for the sake of reform. (Senior official)

> The civil service is poor at knowing what it's there for ... it waits to be told what to do. This is why it isn't effective when it comes to leadership. It has never had to lead. (Senior adviser)

> The thing that most amazed me about working in Whitehall is that no one ever stopped to ask: what and who are we here for? And how are we going to get there? This should be a clear role for non-executive directors, who should constantly be challenging and cajoling departments. Of course, in the current format they don't do this. (Ex senior official)

Weak executive capacity

Second, the lack of a strong centre detracts from Whitehall's ability to set standards, drive improvement or evaluate and manage performance.

> The Cabinet Secretary should be empowered with much greater corporate responsibility – over human resources, pay and so forth – than he currently has. He needs much more in the way of resources. (Ex senior official)

As the creation of 'centres of excellence' demonstrate, there could be important economies of scale from centralising some corporate services and functions – including perhaps human resources, information technology, procurement and commissioning, and financial and knowledge management. More importantly, developing capacity at the centre could, by setting standards, monitoring performance, and providing support, improve attainment for the service across the board. The Delivery Unit and the Strategy Unit could be seen as models for this – as could the newly launched Department Capability Reviews – all of which have helped set standards and build capacity in strategic thinking and public service delivery for the service as a whole. But, despite these efforts, standards and practices still tend to vary hugely across the departments. And, as we show below, performance is poorly monitored and not always adequately managed.

Poor co-ordination

Third, the strongly federal character of the British civil service militates against integrated or joined-up government. Whitehall has long been criticised for being overly departmentalised (Bogdanor 2005). Though cabinet government should, in theory, provide an opportunity for ministers to discuss problems in the round and develop preventative, or at least joined-up, approaches to them, the reality has tended to be rather different, with ministers gaining credibility and reputation 'not so much by their skills at collective ... decision making in Cabinet, but through their successes in managing their departments and departmental infighting' (Bogdanor 2005: 4). Not surprisingly, then, all recent governments have sought to promote cross-departmental co-ordination: Edward Heath appointed a number of super ministries, the second Wilson government established the Joint Approach to Social Policy, while Margaret Thatcher's government favoured Cabinet Committees and single budgets.

New Labour has gone much further than its predecessors, however, in trying to promote 'joined-up government' – or 'JUG' as it became known – in its conviction that complex problems from homelessness through drug addiction to regeneration could not be tackled by functionally organised departments working in isolation. Indeed 'co-ordination and integration' has been described as 'perhaps the central theme' of the Blair government's reform programme (Perri 2005: 45).

Many of our interviewees stressed that real progress has been made on this front. The extensive use of cross-departmental committees, the establishment of jointly owned targets and pooled budgets, and the creation of cross-departmental teams like the Office for Criminal Justice Reform – which reports to the Home Office, Department for Constitutional Affairs and the Attorney General – have led to a more co-ordinated, strategic approach to tackling cross-cutting issues (Mulgan 2005b).

But our interviewees were far from thinking that the challenge had been met. At worse, they argued, Whitehall's strongly departmental structure and culture results in infighting between ministries – or between Downing Street and ministries.

> The centre of government is riddled with turf wars. The Cabinet Secretary could be used to overcome these. (Senior official)

> The tension between No. 10 and [The Treasury] has been responsible for far too many car crashes in Whitehall. (Senior official)

It doesn't help that there are two competing strategic centres in the form of No. 10/Cabinet Office and the Treasury. International governments and UK local government do not suffer from this problem. The relationship and roles are much clearer. (Ex senior official)

But, even when this is avoided, the present system encourages a silo mentality, with problems organised around government and not government around problems.

The federal nature of Whitehall – with its departmental baronies – is a problem for cross-Whitehall governance. It is getting better. We are acting with greater closeness at the top. But barriers remain fairly strong. (Permanent Secretary)

Whitehall still acts too much like a federation. Each department has its own culture and exercises substantial autonomy. Reform, therefore, tends to bite unevenly across Whitehall. We tend to accept those bits of the reform programme we see as sensible and quietly ignore the bits we think are less appropriate or relevant to us. (Permanent Secretary)

No real challenge to the departmental baronialism of Whitehall has been successfully mounted... We tried to transform ministerial portfolios by enhancing the number of horizontal responsibilities over the tradition vertical ones. While some of us wanted to push for a twenty per cent (horizontal) eighty per cent (vertical) split, the reality is that it is more like ninety-eight to two. (Ex senior official)

Performance accountability

Whitehall is fantastically bad at dealing with poor performance. (Senior Private Sector Figure speaking at Reform/KPMG event, December 2005)

If our interviewees tended to see the weaknesses of the centre as a major problem with the civil service, they attached a similar, if not greater, weight to what is, in fact, a related problem – the inadequacy in Whitehall's management of performance and, in particular, its handling of poor performance. The civil service has a poor record when it comes to holding its officials to account for their work.

When it comes to accountability, well-run organisations in any sector tend to have certain key features in common. First, they set clear goals – for the organisation as a whole, for constituent elements within it, and individuals who work for it. Second, they provide the training, support, and

incentives most likely to maximise performance. Third, they supply themselves with accurate information about levels of performance – about the
extent to which units and individuals are achieving their goals. Last, they
learn from the information they have and act on it. This means constantly
reforming and improving structures and processes in light of their performance. It also means promoting and rewarding good performers and

---

Box 3.2 Comparing and contrasting local and central government

A surprising number of the people we spoke to compared central
government unfavourably with the best in local government. Points they
made included:

- The powers concentrated in local authority chief executives ensure that
  councils have a much stronger capacity for corporate leadership than
  does central government.
- Local government is now subject to effective external performance
  assessment in the form of the Comprehensive Performance Assessment
  (CPA), which is widely considered to have driven up standards: the 2005
  CPA showed over 70 per cent of councils as either improving strongly or
  improving well (Audit Commission 2005).
- The chief executive is accountable in his or her own right. He or she
  cannot hide behind the local government equivalent of the convention of
  ministerial responsibility. As one minister said to us, 'In contrast to
  Whitehall, in local government, if a chief executive gets poor a CPA rating,
  the pressure is on for them to go.'
- Despite recent developments putting pressure on the relationship
  between officers and councillors (Solace 2006), there is still a much
  clearer account of the boundary line between the two groups; in
  Whitehall, lines are much more confused.
- The chief executive and senior officers, more generally, are seen as
  working not just for cabinet members or the party in power, but for the
  council, and, beyond that, for the locality as a whole. They don't just look
  upwards, they also look outwards.
- Local authorities are getting increasingly good at partnership-working,
  which, with the advent of Local Strategic Partnerships and Crime and
  Disorder Reduction Partnerships, has become a fact of local government
  (if not central government) life.

Of course, the contrast here is not just of academic interest. It is a source of
real grievance to many working in local government, who wonder why they
should be dictated to by a master who is, in many ways, weaker than the
pupil.

holding those who under-perform to account.

To believe that accountability is important is not necessarily to sub-scribe to a narrowly economist or private sector approach to public management. Not all objectives can be given an economic or even a numerical value. People, perhaps especially those working outside the private sector, are animated by a wide range of motivations and values; a narrow carrot and stick approach will not always be effective – indeed it will often be counter-productive (O'Neill 2005). But, it is important to ensure that people are clear about what is expected of them, and that they know that good performance will be recognised, and poor noted.

How good is the civil service at setting objectives and evaluating and responding to performance? Once again, the service has clearly made progress in many respects. The creation of Public Service Agreements in 1998, and the requirement that departments draw up five-year strategies have helped ensure that the service is much more clearly focused on prior-ities and clear about responsibilities than was once the case. More than 90 per cent of senior civil servants in a recent survey reported, 'I am clear what my organisation is trying to achieve' (Cabinet Office 2005). This is an impressive finding by any standards. The new capability reviews, moreover, should help identify under-performing departments and encourage their improvement.

But many of our interviewees complained that Whitehall is poor at holding mandarins to account – that too often no consequences follow on from failure. Ministers were particularly concerned about this.

> There is simply no price for failure in Whitehall. No price whatso-ever. It is this anomaly that really makes the civil service stand out in comparison to the rest of the public sector. (Minister)

An ex-minister we interviewed put the point in more mischievous terms:

> The most staggering thing about Whitehall is the complete lack of accountability. I would like to write a report evaluating what has gone wrong with the spate of disastrous civil service-led IT procure-ment programmes. I would include an Appendix listing all those officials who have been sacked as a result of these failures. It would be a blank page! (Ex-minister)

But it was not just ministers who complained about poor line management and weak accountability in Whitehall. One civil servant, for instance, sug-gested that the service suffered from an ethos of 'collegiality', with the result that lines of responsibility are ill-defined:

> Whitehall's culture, at times, breeds an unhelpful collegiality. When it comes to running and managing the civil service, then much of this collegiality needs disposing of... Take the new Permanent

Secretaries' Management Group – we can't all sit on it. Collegiality should not be confused with corporacy – they are different things. We need more of the latter and less of the first. (Permanent Secretary)

Others offered frank views on the ineffectiveness of internal accountability:

Internal performance scrutiny is not taken too seriously. The performance partnership agreements[12] were effectively a self-evaluation process, with Permanent Secretaries writing letters to themselves. (Senior official)

The civil service is beginning to put the mechanisms in place – things have moved on since the days of having a chat over a glass of sherry – but it still lacks the culture to really implement effective performance management. Mandarins are clubby and do not really enjoy this sort of thing. (Ex senior adviser)

As a group, Permanent Secretaries have managed to duck accountability. A number of recent changes [PSAs, PPAs and other initiatives] are beginning to change things, but it needs to be made stronger. Permanent secretaries should be held to account for making sure that their departments are 'fit for purpose', and that they have the right capabilities in place ... we do need to find a mechanism for much greater and rigorous scrutiny of Permanent Secretary performance. I think it is very difficult to argue against the logic that this be a form of external scrutiny. (Permanent Secretary)

Others argued that the rapidity with which civil servants move from post to post not only (as we have suggested) undermines institutional learning and memory, but ensures that mandarins can escape responsibility for their decisions:

For most programmes, officials know that they won't be there to face the music. This engenders a culture that does not prize accountability. (Senior public sector leader)

[In Whitehall] poor performers are not removed but are moved around. Doing this is a complete disaster and lies behind many problems. (Senior public sector leader)

Several of the people we spoke to, moreover, were highly critical of the absence of any rigorous external assessment of Whitehall performance. As Sir Michael Bichard has argued, this is all the more surprising given the Government's belief in the importance of subjecting other public bodies to rigorous scrutiny. Perhaps the leading weakness of the civil service, he has suggested, is:

A continuing lack of accountability at personal and organisation (or departmental) level – exacerbated by the failure of the NAO [National Audit Office] and the PAC [Public Accounts Committee] to hold the machine effectively to account. It is odd to read pre-election ODPM literature celebrating the improved performance of local government: 'The evidence from our research shows very clearly that much of the impetus for improvement in recent years has come from central government policies and (external) inspection' … Well, if so much has been achieved by inspection and external assessment, why is there so little evidence that the government is prepared to apply similar methods to the civil service? … Even the internal reformers seem to baulk at the prospect of external scrutiny. (Bichard 2005: 5)

One Permanent Secretary noted that, even where Permanent Secretaries are subject to external assessment, problems remain:

The PAC can be very difficult, but it is not hard-edged accountability … we are not fired as a result of a bad performance. Indeed, appearing before the PAC doesn't change the price of fish! (Permanent Secretary)

The failure to hold civil servants to adequate account is particularly striking, given that they are increasingly being set clear objectives. Where once they were expected simply to advise ministers and administer their business, they are now expected to meet 'delivery targets'. But this, as several of our interviewees pointed out, should make it easier to hold them to account (see Chapter 5).

The emphasis on 'delivery' has serious implications for civil service–minister relations. I think it requires a different relationship. Ministers must set clearly defined objectives for their Permanent Secretaries and senior officials and then they should let them get on and deliver it – and be held to account. There must be much less meddling from ministers and in return we should have a more effective and accountable civil service. But at the moment this relationship is far too blurred – ministers intervene too much and move the goalposts. (Senior public sector leader)

Indeed, we detected a growing acceptance from within the civil service that it should now be subjected to greater external assessment. The view expressed by this Permanent Secretary was typical of what we heard:

We should be externally assessed … the truth is that if [external scrutiny] is good enough for Doncaster Council then it's good enough for the Home Office. I don't have a problem with the accountability laser focused on me. (Permanent Secretary)

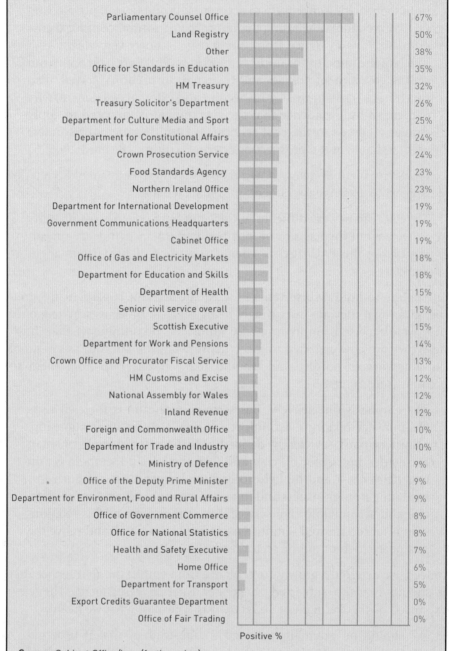

Figure 3.2 Percentage of senior civil service who believe that poor performance is dealt with effectively, by department

Department	Positive %
Parliamentary Counsel Office	67%
Land Registry	50%
Other	38%
Office for Standards in Education	35%
HM Treasury	32%
Treasury Solicitor's Department	26%
Department for Culture Media and Sport	25%
Department for Constitutional Affairs	24%
Crown Prosecution Service	24%
Food Standards Agency	23%
Northern Ireland Office	23%
Department for International Development	19%
Government Communications Headquarters	19%
Cabinet Office	19%
Office of Gas and Electricity Markets	18%
Department for Education and Skills	18%
Department of Health	15%
Senior civil service overall	15%
Scottish Executive	15%
Department for Work and Pensions	14%
Crown Office and Procurator Fiscal Service	13%
HM Customs and Excise	12%
National Assembly for Wales	12%
Inland Revenue	12%
Foreign and Commonwealth Office	10%
Department for Trade and Industry	10%
Ministry of Defence	9%
Office of the Deputy Prime Minister	9%
Department for Environment, Food and Rural Affairs	9%
Office of Government Commerce	8%
Office for National Statistics	8%
Health and Safety Executive	7%
Home Office	6%
Department for Transport	5%
Export Credits Guarantee Department	0%
Office of Fair Trading	0%

Source: Cabinet Office/ippr (forthcoming)

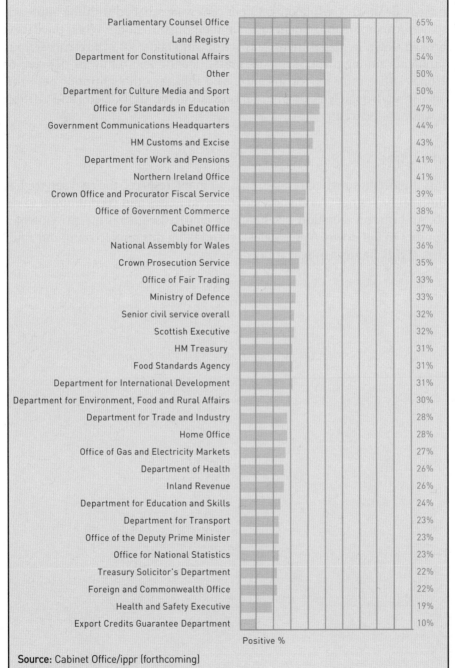

Figure 3.3 Percentage of senior civil service who are satisfied with the approach to performance management, by department

Department	Positive %
Parliamentary Counsel Office	65%
Land Registry	61%
Department for Constitutional Affairs	54%
Other	50%
Department for Culture Media and Sport	50%
Office for Standards in Education	47%
Government Communications Headquarters	44%
HM Customs and Excise	43%
Department for Work and Pensions	41%
Northern Ireland Office	41%
Crown Office and Procurator Fiscal Service	39%
Office of Government Commerce	38%
Cabinet Office	37%
National Assembly for Wales	36%
Crown Prosecution Service	35%
Office of Fair Trading	33%
Ministry of Defence	33%
Senior civil service overall	32%
Scottish Executive	32%
HM Treasury	31%
Food Standards Agency	31%
Department for International Development	31%
Department for Environment, Food and Rural Affairs	30%
Department for Trade and Industry	28%
Home Office	28%
Office of Gas and Electricity Markets	27%
Department of Health	26%
Inland Revenue	26%
Department for Education and Skills	24%
Department for Transport	23%
Office of the Deputy Prime Minister	23%
Office for National Statistics	23%
Treasury Solicitor's Department	22%
Foreign and Commonwealth Office	22%
Health and Safety Executive	19%
Export Credits Guarantee Department	10%

Positive %

Source: Cabinet Office/ippr (forthcoming)

The theme of poor accountability, which came out so strongly in our interviews, is confirmed by some startling data in the SCS staff survey obtained by ippr. Just 16 per cent of the SCS felt that poor performance was adequately dealt with, while only 33 per cent were satisfied with the approach to performance management taken in their organisation.[13] When the data is broken down by department – as set out in Figure 3.2 – it reveals serious problems among most, if not all, major departments. Only six per cent of Home Office officials, for instance, said that they thought poor performance was adequately dealt with; for officials in the MOD, Defra and ODPM, it was nine per cent.

In summary

It is important to reiterate again that, in many respects, the civil service has built on its strengths and addressed its weaknesses and is continuing to do so. And our presentation has naturally emphasised areas where Whitehall appears to fall down. Nevertheless, even taking this into account, our findings highlight areas of real concern.

4 Who governs Whitehall? The governance vacuum

> As a general rule, every executive function, whether superior or inferior, should be the appointed duty of some given individual. It is apparent to the world who did everything and through whose default anything was left undone. Responsibility is null and void when nobody knows who is responsible. (John Stuart Mill, 1861, quoted in Lupson and Partington 2005)

We have been suggesting that, despite its strengths, the civil service is under-performing in a number of important respects. In this chapter, we argue that the roots of many of Whitehall's problems can be traced to the way it is governed, to the constitutional conventions that determine who at the top of the service is responsible for what, and how they are held to account. First, we explore briefly the principles by which the senior civil service is governed at present. Then we explain what we think is wrong with these, highlighting the ambiguities and confusions they throw up. Finally we lay out some of the connections between these and the weaknesses we identified in the last chapter.

Box 4.1 Recent developments in governance and accountability in the private, public and corporate sectors

Governance has been defined as 'the systems and processes concerned with ensuring the overall direction, effectiveness, supervision and accountability of an organisation' (Cornforth 2003).

Some theorists prefer the language of accountability to that of governance, making a distinction between *ex-ante* and *ex-post* accountability. Briefly put, *ex-ante* accountability involves setting the direction of an organisation – its mission and objectives. *Ex-post* accountability is about scrutinising the performance of an organisation and making sure it conducts itself properly and, as far as possible, delivers on its objectives.

Whatever language is used, there is widespread agreement among management experts that the way an organisation is governed or held to account is an important determinant in its performance. It is hardly surprising, therefore, that we have seen a drive over the last decades, to

---

encourage or oblige organisations in every sector to sharpen up their governance.

Most sectors, public, private or voluntary, now have codes that lay out what is expected of those charged with governing organisations, and advise on best practice. Housing associations have a detailed code prepared by the National Housing Federation. Co-operatives UK have the Corporate Governance Code of Best Practice, and charities, the recently issued Good Governance Code (*Good Governance: a Code for the Voluntary and Community Sector* (2005)). In the public sector, there is the new Good Governance Standard for Public Services. And the private sector has its 2004 Combined Code on Corporate Governance, which builds on the work of Cadbury, Greenbury and Higgs.

Central government has, ironically, often led the drive to improve the way organisations are governed – and is constantly reforming the accountability systems of public organisations. Local government is a case in point. The Local Government Act 2000 required local authorities to abandon the traditional committee-based system, replacing it with an executive model and a system of scrutiny for backbench councillors. The governance of the civil service, however, has remained largely untouched (see Chapter 5).

Of course, the governance of the civil service is unusual in two respects. First, its fundamental rules are mainly conventional rather than written. Second, they form part of Britain's still largely unwritten constitution. This last characteristic is an important factor in explaining why those charged with reforming the civil service have tended to shy away from altering the way it is governed. Reforming Whitehall's architecture of accountability involves reforming an important part of the constitution.

Whitehall: governing conventions, principles and ambiguities

How, then, is Whitehall governed? How are roles defined, goals set, and responsibilities apportioned at the top of the civil service? And who ensures that the service as a whole, its constituent elements and its leaders are performing as well as they could?

As already indicated, it is hard to find an authoritative account of the principles lying behind Whitehall's governance arrangements or the arrangements themselves. The Northcote-Trevelyan report took the advantages of a permanent and non-partisan civil service responsible to Parliament as so obvious as not to need much articulation or defence (Northcote and Trevelyan 1854: 2). A century and a half has passed since then, but the precise roles and responsibilities of the civil service – or of ministers – have never been formally laid down in statute, nor is there any legal definition of a civil servant (Plowden 1994; Marsh *et al* 2001). Nevertheless, a number of conventions or principles laid down in the 19th century are generally seen as fundamental. Here, following Bogdanor (2003), we distinguish four: ministerial responsibility; non-partisanship; admission by open competition; and promotion by ability.

Ministerial responsibility

This, perhaps the most important convention, states that civil servants exist to serve ministers in advising on and executing government policy. But ministers – and ministers alone – are accountable to Parliament, and, ultimately, to the electorate, for both the operation of the civil service and for the policies they ask it to execute.[14]

Ministerial responsibility – to use Bagehot's memorable phrase – acts as the 'buckle' of the constitution, by linking the executive to the legislature. Ministerial responsibility defines and shapes the relationship between ministers and officials, the civil service and parliament and the outside world. It, more than anything else, moulds civil service behaviour, culture and identity.

Non-partisanship

This convention stipulates that civil servants should serve all governments of whatever political colour with equal dedication.

Admission by open competition

This convention dictates that recruitment into the civil service should be according to the merits of the candidate, objectively defined through examination or other formal procedure. It forbids anyone being appointed to the service through the purchase of their office, or on grounds of their connections, political or familial, with those in power.

Promotion by ability

This convention says that posts in the civil service should go to those best qualified to meet the demands that accompany them.

Together, these conventions formed the basis of what is often called the 'deal' lying at the heart of the relationship between ministers and officials (Wilson, quoted in Plowden 1994). Crudely, this amounts to an agreement that 'civil servants advise, ministers decide' (Smith 1999). Ministers get the service of an expert and dedicated cadre of non-partisan and anonymous advisers and administrators. Civil servants get ministers who value their expertise, respect their advice and support the ethos of the service. Importantly, the 'deal' rested on a shared understanding of the respective roles and responsibilities of ministers and officials. It is a very British arrangement – a largely unspoken 'gentlemen's agreement', assuming the good character and mutual understanding of all those involved.

What is wrong, then, with these arrangements? The problem lies with their deep ambiguity – the lack of clearly defined relations of accountability – and their increasing unsuitability to today's world. Indeed, it is a striking, but little observed, feature of all these conventions that each can be, and frequently is, represented as advancing the authority of ministers and, ultimately, Parliament, *or* as advancing the independence of the civil service, depending on circumstance and the perspective of those making the argument.

Take ministerial responsibility. At first sight this convention seems obviously to give Westminster authority over Whitehall. Yet, the convention also limits Parliament's power to hold civil servants directly to account. If civil servants, it is argued, are going to be able to serve ministers of all parties faithfully and effectively, it is vital that they do not become associated, in the mind of the public or politicians, with one particular set of party political policies. For this reason, they have to remain anonymous and insulated. Parliament cannot effectively hold them to account or scrutinise their conduct. (Indeed, Bagehot insisted that the civil service should be protected from the outside interference of the 'busy bodies and the crotchet makers of the House and country' (Bagehot 1867).)

Or take the conventions around recruitment, promotion and impartiality. Sometimes they are presented as ensuring that ministers have at their disposal an expert and impartial service, willing and able to do their bidding. On another interpretation, however, these conventions work to place limits on ministers' powers, by giving the civil service a degree of freedom from ministerial control. They ensure that ministers cannot formally influence civil servants or politicise the service.

The governance vacuum

It is hardly surprising, in the light of the ambiguity of the governing conventions outlined above, if lines of accountability at the top of Whitehall are ill-defined. Below, we single out three respects in which accountability is particularly weak or confused.

Civil servant accountability

First, the ambiguities in the civil service's governing conventions leave civil servants only very weakly accountable to anybody but themselves. The principles that all decisions taken by the civil service are decisions of the minister insulate civil servants from parliamentary or public scrutiny. As AL Lowell put it in 1908, 'the permanent official, like the King, can do no wrong. Both are shielded by the responsibility of the minister' (quoted in

Box 4.2 Ministerial responsibility

The principle of ministerial responsibility is capable of being given more or less rigid interpretation. But, for most of the history of the civil service, it has been given a very rigid interpretation indeed. On this understanding, the civil service has no independent existence at all – it is simply there to serve the government of the day. As Sir Robert Armstrong, head of the civil service, put it in his famous 1985 memorandum laying down rules of conduct for officials:

> The civil service has no constitutional personality separate and apart from the government of the day ... the duty of the individual civil servant is first and foremost to the Minister of the Crown who is in charge of the Department in which he or she is serving. (Evidence to the Treasury and Civil Service Select Committee 1985-86)

Indeed the *Carltona* principle – a derivative of ministerial responsibility – demands that when civil servants speak in public, for instance in court, they speak not for themselves, but only on behalf of the minister. They are said to lack a 'constitutional personality', something that is reinforced by the so-called *Osmotherly Rules*. Designed to preserve the principle of ministerial responsibility (and redrafted in 2005), these rules protect officials from public accountability and enable ministers to decide who represents them before select committees, and to control what officials say – after all, they are only speaking on behalf of the minister.

Not everyone subscribes to as rigorous an interpretation of the doctrine of ministerial responsibility as the one laid out in the Armstrong Memorandum. And political/constitutional practice certainly appears to depart from Armstrong's principles. (See Plowden 1994: 113-114; and Marquand, 2004.)

In reality, civil servants have long been publicly accountable, in certain limited respects, and the trend is for them to become more so. Permanent Secretaries have, since 1926, had to answer, in their role as accounting officers, to the Public Accounts Committee. Though the exact standing of chief executives of Next Steps agencies is unclear, they are generally recognised, especially where non-contentious agencies are concerned, as being at least semi-independent civil servants, who are directly answerable to Parliament in at least some circumstances (Woodhouse 2003: 285 and 316-321).

cont. next page

The advent of the Ombudsman to deal with maladministration also provided a direct source of external scrutiny of government departments, and is thus regarded by some as an incursion into the doctrine of ministerial responsibility (Fry 1970); although, the senior civil service has largely escaped the scrutiny of the Ombudsman. Moves, moreover, to increase public and parliamentary access to government information – especially since the introduction of freedom of information (FOI) – have also weakened ministerial responsibility and diminished civil service anonymity: Parliament and the public can now often go behind ministers' backs and get information about the civil service – and about the conduct of named civil servants – for themselves. And there have been cases where public inquiries or parliamentary reports have named and blamed civil service officials (Woodhouse 2003: 293).

Nevertheless, the principle of ministerial responsibility remains, in the absence of any convention or statute to replace it, a very powerful one that still shapes relations between Whitehall and Westminster (Bogdanor 2003; Flinders 2005; Rhodes 2005). Civil servants are not held to account in any systematic way. Select committees are often frustrated in their inquiries by the stricture that they should not inquire into the conduct of officials. As one official said to us: '[The Osmotherly Rules] mean that select committees only get half the story from us rather than the full picture.' Importantly, the Next Steps reforms deliberately sought to preserve untouched the principle of ministerial responsibility, in that ministers and ministers alone remained accountable for the actions performed by both the department and its agencies.

Senior civil servants, especially Permanent Secretaries, see their role almost exclusively in terms of serving the minister of the day – ministerial responsibility remains a 'brute fact of life' (Rhodes 2005). In short, as Diana Woodhouse has put it, 'Despite its inadequacies and concerns about its effectiveness ... [ministerial responsibility] continues to permeate the procedures and language of the House of Commons, underpin the structure of government and govern the relationship between ministers and civil servants' (2003: 283).

Bogdanor 2003). They act in the name of the minister and are only accountable through him or her.

Yet the conventions of recruitment and advancement on merit and non-partisanship give ministers themselves only very limited powers over civil servants – decisions over the appointment, removal, promotion and demotion, or remuneration rest with the civil service, not with ministers. In other words, Whitehall is not subject to *external* accountability, nor is it subject to effective forms of *internal* accountability, since ministers are prohibited from holding them to account in a meaningful way. Instead, it is largely accountable to itself.

The same conventions arguably encourage a tendency to view ministerial involvement in civil service affairs as unwarranted or even unconstitutional 'interference'. Ministers very rarely get involved in internal civil service reorganisation or reform. Indeed, ministers we spoke to complained that internal reorganisations of departments often took place without their consent. Often, they are precluded from becoming involved, even though they would have to take responsibility for any repercussions from such changes. Indeed, some would argue that the conventions help foster a certain Whitehall wariness of politicians and the political process. For all of their talk about being servants of ministers, Whitehall officials, some have complained, are only too eager to say 'No, Minister' (Bichard 2005: 6).

Reflecting on this state of affairs, ex-Home Secretary, David Blunkett recently complained:

> '… Ministers are precluded from a direct role in ensuring that the structure to deliver the policies that Parliament has voted on or where Ministers with executive power to implement, are capable or appropriate to do so. Other than their own private office – where options will be offered to them – and where, in consultation with the Civil Service Commission, Permanent Secretaries have the wisdom to do so, they are excluded from appointments, promotion or, in the case of gross incompetence, any role in recommending disciplinary action. Civil servants are entirely dependent on, and managerially responsible to, their senior "permanent" officials, not Ministers.' (Blunkett 2006)

Ministerial accountability

Second, the ambiguities in the civil service's governing conventions mean that ministers are also insufficiently accountable. Of course, there are important respects in which they can be held to account. The Ministerial Code makes it plain they answer to the Prime Minister – and no one could deny that prime ministers use their powers to appoint and remove ministers with dizzying frequency. (We have had 11 Home Secretaries since 1979, giving them a tenure of less than two-and-a-half years each.) They are also accountable to Parliament and its select committees. Yet, Parliament only has limited powers of scrutiny and even less ability to force the resignation of a minister; despite the importance of resignation as 'an essential component of the control of government' and 'the final stage in the process of accountability', very few ministers resign without first being pushed to do so by their prime minister (Woodhouse 2003: 295).

Civil servants themselves, moreover, have very little formal power over ministers – and the conventions dictating that they cannot speak for themselves in public means that they are in a weak position if a minister insists, as they sometimes do, on blaming civil servants for administrative failures. Ministers are often accused, for instance, of making policy on the hoof or imposing initiatives without sufficient care for their consequences. Yet, the service has very little scope to resist this sort of behaviour or promote better practice. Civil servants can now directly report alleged breaches of the Civil Service Code to the Civil Service Commissioners, but this option is generally viewed as a last resort, and is rarely used. For instance, between 2005 and 2006 no appeals were made to the Commissioners (Civil Service Commissioners 2006).

Indeed, the convention of ministerial responsibility itself can, as has often been pointed out, provide protection for ministers (Woodhouse 2003: 328). Everyone now agrees that the doctrine that ministers are accountable for everything that goes on in their departments cannot be taken literally – they cannot be, as Herbert Morrison once claimed they were, responsible for every postage stamp that goes on every letter (Plowden 1994; Barberis 1998; Darwell 2006). This concession, however, makes it all too easy to refine the convention almost out of existence. Because ministers are said to be accountable for everything, they end up being accountable for almost nothing (see Box 4.3).

> Accountability is the central issue, but it is difficult. The current arrangements are fraught with ambiguities – and remember this suits both sides. The accountability fudge we have now protects ministers and officials. Ministers can say 'not me, guv', while officials hide behind them. This is not in the interest of effective government. (Senior official)

Lack of clarity in Cabinet Secretary–Permanent Secretary relations

Third, relations between the Cabinet Secretary and Permanent Secretaries are ill-defined. According to the principle of ministerial responsibility, Permanent Secretaries – and the civil servants in their department – answer ultimately to the minister at the head of the department, and also to Parliament, in their capacity as accounting officers. Yet, the Cabinet Secretary also has some claim to authority (as does the Treasury and its Permanent Secretary although the latter wields much less influence over the civil service now than in the past). The Cabinet Secretary, after all, is the 'Head' of the civil service, and held to be responsible, with the Minister for the Cabinet Office and the Prime Minister, for its overall performance.

The Cabinet Secretary is expected to lead on civil service reform. And the centre, in the guise of the Cabinet Secretary, Prime Minister, Treasury and/or

Chancellor, has been taking an evermore active role in setting departmental targets, and monitoring and managing performance. If Permanent Secretaries are, then, formally accountable to their ministers, they have, in practice, to answer increasingly to Downing Street, the Cabinet Office and the Treasury. Lines of accountability at the top of the civil service look like a bowl of spaghetti.

Box 4.3 Who is in charge around here?

The ambiguity at the heart of Whitehall's accountability regime is never more evident than when a department finds itself in trouble. Rarely is anyone clear about what is expected of civil servants or ministers in cases of administrative failure. Civil servants scarcely ever resign, and are rarely demoted or dismissed (Stanley 2006). The general practice, if things go wrong, is to move them sideways. Ministers, similarly, do not often resign without first being pushed – and only very rarely because of departmental or policy failure (Woodhouse 2002). True, they are often removed from their post, but often there is little clarity as to why. There is, in fact, disagreement on what is entailed by 'ministerial responsibility', and ministers set on remaining in power will find the constitutional writers full of handy distinctions between 'accountability' (giving an explanation) and 'responsibility' (liability) – or between 'explanatory', 'remedial', 'supervisory' and 'sacrificial' accountability (Marshall 1989; Barberis 1998; Woodhouse 2003).

The lack of clarity about who is responsible for what in government, moreover, fosters suspicion and resentment all round. This is evident from our own interviews, with ministers complaining that they always have to take responsibility even when they are not culpable, and civil servants complaining that ministers never take responsibility, even when they should.

> There is a real frustration in Whitehall ... that officials will often get blamed for things, including by ministers who use them as a decoy, but never have the opportunity to put their case. With a more ruthless and predatory media, this problem is growing. In fact, I would quite like greater accountability as it would allow me to put my side of the story forward. There is a problem at the moment in that Permanent Secretaries are increasingly being pilloried in the press for things – often highly misrepresented events – that they are not

cont. next page

allowed to react to or answer back. Perhaps we should be able to come out and make public statements. (Senior official)

Writing in *The Guardian*, Polly Toynbee reported: 'One cabinet minister claims to know of no case of a civil servant being fired or demoted, or a Permanent Secretary taking the rap, even when ministers have fallen on their words unjustly' (Toynbee 2006). It is alleged that David Blunkett, then Home Secretary, complained bitterly to his Permanent Secretary: 'My minister has resigned but your man has stayed put', after Beverely Hughes was forced to resign over a failure at the Sheffield office of the Immigration and Nationality Directorate (Blunkett 2006).

Changing times

It is arguable that, in earlier times, these ambiguities did not matter much. The 'Whitehall Deal' worked well. Throughout the 19th and into the early 20th century, the British Government was, after all, a small, face-to-face organisation dealing with relatively simple tasks. Departments were even smaller. The 18th-century Home Secretary Lord Shelbourne presided over a Home Office that employed one clerk and 10 civil servants (Flinders 2005). By 1913, the Home Office still had only 28 staff – one Permanent Secretary, one under-secretary, two legal under-secretaries, six assistant secretaries and 18 clerks (Pellow 1982). In these circumstances, it made some sense to claim that ministers were personally responsible for everything that went on in their department. It was reasonable to believe that ministers would respect civil servants' neutrality and objectivity, and that civil servants would act on ministers' wishes. And it was sensible to hope that, if things went wrong, those involved would be able sort their differences out between them.[15]

Times, however, have changed. To begin with, central government and its agencies have grown immeasurably, and the challenges they face are much more complex. Today, the Home Office employs over 70,000 officials working in the department and a range of arms-length agencies and Non-Departmental Public Bodies (NDPBs) (Flinders 2005).

Moreover, as the service has grown, and as a greater attachment has been given to managing operations, delivering services and promoting outcomes, so civil servants have been given, or taken on, greater managerial independence – a development well illustrated by the hiving off of many parts of the service into quasi-independent agencies in the 1990s. To suggest that ministers must remain accountable for all the actions of this vast and sprawling machine defies common sense. Equally, it is not simply a case that Whitehall's governing conventions no longer fit with the demands of

21st-century government, we would also contend that they actively serve to undermine the ability of the civil service to perform the new roles assigned to it.

At the same time, party politics has, if anything, become more adversarial, and the Opposition is quick to grab any opportunity to criticise ministers and their civil servants. The media has become less respectful and more sceptical, and the public less trusting. Modern organisations, especially organisations as important and high-profile as Whitehall, need to be able to set out precisely who is responsible for what, and to demonstrate that those responsible are properly held to account. In these circumstances, the old arrangements look gravely anachronistic.

Many of our interviewees complained about the inadequacy of Whitehall's governance arrangements, especially the lack of clear lines of accountability. Indeed, many felt that the situation was getting worse:

> Presently, we lack clarification on the respective roles and responsibilities of ministers and mandarins. The Code of Good Practice [HM Treasury 2005] attempts to clear things up but ultimately fails to do so. It fudges the whole issue ... (Permanent Secretary)

> Although I think that the civil service is in the best shape I have known it during my career, I would say that clarifying the roles of ministers and officials is the major unresolved constitutional question. It is a question that has been deliberately left untouched – the Pandora's Box that now needs opening. (Permanent Secretary)

> There is a muddle over ministerial and senior civil service roles and responsibilities – this is beginning to bite and become and a live issue. (Permanent Secretary)

Accountability and performance in Whitehall

> Clarifying and sharpening accountability will significantly improve performance and delivery. (HM Treasury/Public Services Productivity Panel 2002)

We have been contending that Whitehall's governance arrangements are fundamentally unclear. But does this matter? We suggest that it does. Indeed, we argue that the weaknesses identified in the last chapter have their roots in the governance vacuum at the top of Whitehall – a position nicely articulated by one of the officials we interviewed.

> Whitehall's culture and way of thinking stems from its constitutional position and its relationship with ministers... You won't achieve sig-

nificant reform unless the constitutional position of the service is addressed. (Senior official)

To a considerable extent, the connections between governance and performance are obvious. If, as we have suggested, governance is concerned with both defining an organisation's mission and setting well-thought-through and challenging goals for it, and scrutinising and managing its performance, it follows that organisations that are poorly governed are likely to display:

- a lack of clear sense of purpose or direction
- ill-defined objectives
- a lack of clarity as to whom the organisation should serve
- poor co-ordination
- weak process of scrutiny and performance management
- limited capacity for change and reform.

Most of these charges can be levelled, as we have suggested, at Whitehall. But if there are fairly self-evident links between governance and organisational performance, the form these links take inevitably varies from organisation to organisation. Below, we set out some of the ways the connections between inadequate governance and effectiveness work in the case of the Whitehall civil service.

Poor performance accountability

The inadequacies in Whitehall's system of governance help explain its relatively weak record when it comes to performance accountability – why, in particular, it is poor at dealing with under-performance. First, the lack of a strong accountability culture at the top of the organisation arguably shapes the culture of the service as a whole. Second, the ambiguities in accountability and the civil service's traditions of self-governance have allowed the service to avoid the sort of external assessment that is now standard for most public organisations. Turkeys do not vote for Christmas.

The result is that there is no real reward for success in Whitehall, and no price for failure. Often, Whitehall does not have to deal with the consequences of its actions.

Why are we poor at delivery? Mainly it's because there aren't any rewards or sanctions for good delivery. (Senior official)

You have to wonder where the real accountability is, by which I mean some effective assessment of achievements and failures. This is the accountability that matters and this is what is really missing. The major difficulty in Whitehall is that as soon as you start trying to make civil servants more accountable you very quickly bump into ministers. A major problem in Britain is that we do not have a coherent account of the boundary line between ministers and officials. (Ex senior official)

Lack of capacity for radical change

As several of our interviewees pointed out, the self-governing character of Whitehall means that it is never placed under external pressure to change – or at least, that it can withstand any pressure that politicians or others attempt to exert on it.

> The most fundamental problem with the civil service is that it is not accountable to anybody. It certainly isn't accountable to ministers. This explains why the pace of change in Whitehall is best described as glacial. (Minister)

> One thing is certain in Whitehall – the pace of change will be slow. Especially when compared to parts of the private sector and local government. There is no agency for driving change. We develop our own reform programme and then are left to get on and implement it. (Permanent Secretary)

Weak leadership

As we saw in the last chapter, many of our interviewees complained that, despite the qualities of many senior officials, Whitehall lacked a strong leadership culture. But then Whitehall's accountability system could hardly be better designed to prevent strong leadership. Ministers, though formally in charge of their departments, rarely make departmental reform a priority. Anyway, given the self-governing character of the civil service there is a limit to the changes politicians can affect.

At the same time, the Permanent Secretaries are discouraged from taking too prominent leadership role themselves – they are, after all, there to provide anonymous service to ministers. In some respects, Cabinet Secretaries find themselves in a still more difficult position. On the one hand they are 'Head of the Home Civil Service'. On the other, they are, like Permanent Secretaries, meant to provide anonymous support to the Prime Minister and Cabinet. Cabinet Secretaries, moreover, have only very limited leverage over departmental Permanent Secretaries. They are first among equals, rather than leaders. In these circumstances, it is not surprising if the civil service sometimes struggles when it comes to corporate leadership – to reflecting on its mission, identifying its objectives, or managing ambitious change.

Politicians want an independent and robust civil service, but they are not prepared to drive the reforms or to articulate a vision. This means that it gets left to the civil service. A key question is why it's so hard for civil servants to drive reform themselves. Should it be the role of the civil service to oversee reform? We have to accept that the civil service finds it very difficult to generate the reform energy needed to change. (Ex senior official)

Civil Service reform is slow-moving and uneven for a number of reasons. The politicians are not interested, and so it is left to the civil service to design and implement a reform programme. But we don't have a unified vision of what we should look like. Therefore, reform takes the form of bits and pieces that have been able to get past thirty-odd Permanent Secretaries. (Permanent Secretary)

For some reason, ministers never value the importance of civil service reform – it just isn't a priority and therefore the civil service is left to get on with things themselves. (Ex senior official)

A central theme to emerge throughout our interviews was the constitutional weakness of the position of the Cabinet Secretary (rather than the Cabinet Secretary himself).

The civil service does not have a chief executive, someone who is responsible for setting the strategic direction of the service, and for organising the government machine so that it is able to deliver. (Ex senior official)

The Cabinet Secretary has no real power base in Whitehall. This is a major weakness. Because Permanent Secretaries are accounting officers in their own right there is no thick line of accountability between the Cabinet Secretary and Permanent Secretaries. This needs changing. Currently, poor performers are eased out in a very traditional mandarin way. It's not an effective approach. I would like to see the Cabinet Secretary have the power to remove Permanent Secretaries. (Permanent Secretary)

The position of the Cabinet Secretary in the British constitution needs reviewing. The Cabinet Secretary should be able to hold Permanent Secretaries and their senior teams to account for their performance, equipped with both sanctions and rewards. The present situation is clearly unsatisfactory. We are asking him to run the civil service solely on the force of his personality. The Cabinet Secretary needs a much stronger institutional basis in order to be effective. (Permanent Secretary)

In many ways, the position of the Cabinet Secretary is the worst job in Whitehall. I wouldn't like the job! It is ... very difficult to move Permanent Secretaries into some sort of manageable corporate entity. (Permanent Secretary)

Poor management
The limitations in the doctrine of ministerial responsibility also contribute in a major way to Whitehall's less than outstanding record when it comes to management and operational delivery. Because decisions drift upwards to the ministers, very often civil servants look to them to lead on operational decisions, but ministers rarely have the time, interest or aptitude for public management. The result is that responsibility for operations falls between the cracks.

Ministerial overload
Perhaps, conversely, the limitations in the way Whitehall is governed also help explain why ministers do not always govern as well as they might. The doctrine of ministerial responsibility means they are overloaded with departmental business, giving them little time to concentrate on policy.[16]

However, it has to be said that the problem of overload does not just stem from civil servants drawing ministers into departmental detail. Ministers, lacking confidence in their civil servants, often feel obliged to take as much control as they can (Toynbee 2006).

Departmentalism
There are obvious connections between the strongly federal character of Whitehall's accountability structure – with Permanent Secretaries being answerable, at least in theory, to their ministers – and Whitehall's tendency to work in departmental silos. An organisation with a stronger centre might find it easier to organise the service around problems and promote really effective joined-up government.

Insularity
Finally, many of our interviewees also suggested that the civil service's governance structure explains another problem with it: its historic, but still abiding, tendency to insularity – its preference for secrecy over openness, its weak traditions when it comes to working with or engaging with the private sector, local government, voluntary organisations or citizens.

This is a case where the convention of ministerial responsibility and the service self-governing character tend to work in the same direction. That it is largely self-governing encourages civil servants to think of themselves as answerable to no one other than the civil service itself – a view encapsulated in William Armstrong's famous dictum, 'I am accountable to my own ideal of a civil servant.' The convention of ministerial responsibility – the convention that the civil service has no personality at all and simply exists to serve ministers and Cabinet – encourages civil servants to focus upwards. Neither convention, however, encourages Whitehall to look outwards: to engage with the public – with the people it is, ultimately, there to serve.

> A real problem in Whitehall is the lack of public focus – despite the rhetoric about how we are here to serve the public, the fact is that everything is centred on serving ministers. (Senior official)

> If engagement is a central objective of the modern government in advanced democracies, then how can you seriously postulate the idea that the civil service can only act or speak on behalf of ministers. It is a preposterous fiction. (Permanent Secretary)

Box 4.4 The impact of Whitehall's governing conventions: a summary

- Respective roles and responsibilities of ministers and officials lack clarity; there is confusion over who does what.
- There is an absence of clear corporate leadership, so detracting from the service's ability to think and act strategically or drive change.
- Civil servants have a weak sense of individual responsibility; there is no tradition of feeling accountable for outcomes – too often there is no price for failure in Whitehall.
- The conventions militate against root and branch change – as a self-governing institution, the civil service can, and in the past always has, avoided fundamental reform; there is no external pressure to change.
- They allow ministers and civil servants to duck and dive behind one another and avoid taking responsibility for their actions.
- They encourage civil servants to focus upwards on ministers, rather than outwards and downwards on civil society organisations and citizens.
- They result in a neglect of managerial and operational matters – the doctrine of ministerial responsibility dictates that ministers are responsible not only for developing and applying policies, but for the strategic management and operations of their departments. Yet, most ministers have little interest and even less capacity in issues of strategic management and operations.
- They promote ministerial overload by drawing ministers into operational details.

---

5 Recommendations for moving forward

So far, we have been identifying problems with the civil service and exploring their interconnection. In this chapter, we discuss reform options and lay out a reform programme.

Our first point is that the priority for Whitehall must now be to reform the way it is governed. This might seem obvious from our arguments in the last two chapters, but it needs stressing, because it is, in some respects, the hardest of options. For one thing, changing the way Whitehall is governed means recasting a part of Britain's unwritten constitution. For another, it will inevitably affect the powers and responsibilities of both mandarins and ministers. All involved are bound to be nervous.

Yet, we argue, this is the only option that will be effective. If past reform efforts have not been as successful as was hoped, it is in large measure just because they avoided tackling the big accountability issues. They focused on what are, from the perspective of our analysis, 'second-order' matters.[17] A further heave of the same sort is unlikely to be any more effective. The key lies not with more of the same, but with ensuring that those at the top of the service have clearly defined roles and responsibilities, and the resources to ensure that they can exercise them.

Two avenues of reform

How, then, could the governance vacuum at the heart of Whitehall be addressed? What should we fill it with?

It is helpful, in thinking about the reform of Whitehall's accountability arrangements, to distinguish between two different approaches that might be taken – though the distinction is a bit artificial, in so far as we suggest ways of combining elements of each.

Politicisation

The first would be to make the doctrine of ministerial responsibility a reality by further politicising Whitehall. This is, arguably, the default option at the moment: in response to a growing frustration with continued problems and under-performance, ministers tend to want to take more power for themselves.

> Many of us feel that we have little control over civil servants at the moment. There needs to be greater ministerial control, though of course any such change would need to put in place effective safeguards. (Minister)

Box 5.1 A reformed civil service?

We have been arguing that Whitehall's governance arrangements, and the constitutional conventions that underpin them, have changed little from the days of Northcote-Trevelyan – that the civil service is run on the basis of an unspoken gentleman's agreement, struck 150 years ago. Some might object that we are caricaturising the civil service, which has, in fact, reformed its governance from within.

Whitehall, for instance, now has a Civil Service Code, introduced in 1996 and recently revised, and a Ministerial Code, established in 1997. The role of the Civil Service Commissioners, established in 1855, has recently been strengthened, so that they can now receive complaints about breaches of the Civil Service Code directly from civil servants (Cabinet Office 2006). Individual departments have gained their own boards, replete with external or 'non-executive' directors. HM Treasury even went so far as to publish a corporate governance code for central government *The Code of Best Practice for Good Governance in Central Government Departments* (HM Treasury 2005).

Finally, the new Cabinet Secretary, Sir Gus O'Donnell, has created a new Permanent Secretaries' Management Group, along with a steering body made up of senior Permanent Secretaries, designed to drive the civil service.

Yet, the effects of these reforms are bound, by their very nature, to be limited, for they leave the fundamental conventions that determine who is responsible for what in Whitehall unchanged. So Commissioners, boards, even Parliament, are all supervising a deeply ambiguous set of relationships. The new corporate governance code, Code of Good Governance, for instance, carefully avoids clarity on the central issue of ministerial–civil servant relations, with the result that it cannot be used in apportioning responsibility or addressing disputes over responsibility when these arise. Many of our interviewees were highly critical of these arrangements, and departmental boards in particular:

> The Civil Service Management Board is a complete joke. And an expensive one, since it means that Whitehall is deprived of any collective sense of purpose. (Ex senior official)

> Whitehall boards lack purpose ... the board is not actually collectively responsible for anything. They are basically an advisory

> panel for the Permanent Secretary. (Senior public sector figure)
>
> Boards are a complete anomaly. Nothing more than a vehicle for Permanent Secretary patronage. (Ex adviser)

Under this option, ministers would be given greater authority over the appointment and removal of senior civil servants and the strategic direction and internal organisation of the service. Ministers would, in turn, take on a real, rather than a 'formal', responsibility for civil service performance. That does not mean that they would have to be responsible for everything – they could give appointees clear objectives and responsibilities. Nevertheless, ministers would, in effect, gain greater control over and responsibility for every aspect of the civil service.

Where this route is followed politicians generally appoint people who share their broad outlook and these appointees leave their offices when the government that appointed them loses power. As indicated above, this approach is not untried. Indeed, 'By the end of the twentieth century,' Vernon Bogdanor has observed, 'the British civil service was almost alone … in remaining unpoliticised in its upper reaches' (Bogdanor 2003: 238). There is, moreover, much to be said in favour of this approach. It keeps authority firmly in the hands of elected politicians. And it provides the civil service with fresh blood where, arguably, it needs it most – at the top.

Despite the arguments that can be made in its favour, however, we do not recommend the further politicisation of the civil service. Below, we lay out the considerations that have led us to reject this option.

- Politicisation is unsuited to Britain's constitutional settlement. The absence of a formal separation of powers ensures that Britain already has a very strong executive. Extensive politicisation of the civil service would increase its strength still further. A politically neutral civil service constitutes an important check and balance in British government, which we want to preserve. Further, we are not convinced that, where Westminster-style governments have moved to a more overtly politicised system – such as in Australia, or for a brief spell in Canada – that it has worked. (See Savoie 1994; Weller and Young 2001; Aucion 2006.)

We acknowledge that constitutional safeguards could be introduced to oversee a system of politicisation. Parliamentary committees, like US congressional committees, could, for instance, be asked to approve appointees, but we believe that these processes – as a general rule – are cumbersome, time consuming and would not prove effective.

- Ministers already complain, reasonably enough, that they are overloaded with responsibilities and do not have enough time to focus on the important policy decisions they are elected to make. Politicisation, however, would further exacerbate ministerial and prime ministerial overload. Politicisation, moreover, demands a lot from ministers. It assumes they have the 'knowhow' and 'expertise' to appoint the right type of person to the job of running major departments of state. Some will not find this a challenge, but others, and in our view the majority, will. Their skills lie elsewhere. We think it better to leave the management of departments to the civil service, on the provision that it is fit for this task.

- The rapidity with which British ministers move in and out of posts would create real problems for a politicised system – at least if political appointees were to follow ministers. Indeed, it would be a recipe for administrative chaos. One way round this would be for the Prime Minister, rather than ministers, to appoint senior officials. But this would dramatically increase the power of the Prime Minister and put excessive demands on him or her. Prime ministers already have enough to occupy them without having to appoint and answer for an army of political officers.

The second model, one we broadly favour, seeks to build on the civil services traditions of objectivity and neutrality, by giving civil servants greater responsibility for the day-to-day operations of the service, while clarifying the prerogatives and duties of ministers – and increasing the accountability of both. We favour, in short, recasting the convention of ministerial responsibility by making Whitehall directly accountable for the delivery of government policy, while protecting ministers' roles with regard to directing policy. And we favour creating an external governing body, appointed by and answerable to Parliament, dedicated to setting strategic direction for Whitehall, appointing the civil service Head, overseeing performance, setting standards for both civil servants and ministers, and managing the division of responsibility between them.

In short, we recommend the creation of:

- A **Civil Service Governing Body**, responsible for civil service strategy and values, appointing its head, supervising its performance, and laying out, and policing, the roles and responsibilities of ministers and mandarins.
- A **Civil Service Executive**, led by an empowered Head of the Civil Service, tasked with appointing senior civil servants, running core corporate functions, driving innovation, managing performance, and orchestrating and overseeing cross-departmental working.

We believe this model has a number of merits. First, it has the great virtue of building on what remain very valuable traditions of civil service independence impartiality and integrity, and on the trust that the public still largely has in Whitehall. Trust is an increasingly valuable commodity – it should not be squandered lightly. Second, it provides a way of ending the old Whitehall tradition of self-governance, and offers a way of making both civil servants, and to some extent ministers, more accountable for their work. Third, this model is most likely to encourage strategic leadership and long-term thinking on the part of the civil service, and ensure that it becomes a more outward looking organisation, with better networks into the private, voluntary and public sectors and communities. Fourth, it increases the power of the centre in relation to departments, bringing an end to the departmentalism that has afflicted Whitehall for too long.

There are two main objections to this approach to reforming the civil service. The first is that the distinction between 'operations' and 'policy' on which it rests is unworkable. The second is that it would represent a dilution of the power of democratically elected government. Before turning to lay out our recommendations in detail, we respond to each of these.

The policy operations distinction

As we have suggested, over the last few decades civil servants have gained new responsibilities, especially operational responsibilities, and an increased degree of managerial independence. We argue that it is time for government to recognise and respond to this development: instead of politicians being held publicly responsible for every corner of the civil service, the convention of ministerial responsibility should be revised and civil servants should be held externally responsible for operational matters and other matters for which they have been given clearly defined responsibility.

Some politicians and some public management specialists argue, however, that the distinction between a sphere of 'policy' and a sphere of 'operations' is so hazy as to be inapplicable in practice (see Public Service Committee 1996; Straw quoted in Drewry 2004). They have a point. Operational difficulties may be a consequence of badly designed policy. Conversely, a good policy will suffer if poorly implemented. (Criminal justice legislation, to take just one example, that has the effect of increasing the prison population is likely to make it harder for those running the prison service to meet a range of operational objectives like those around reducing re-offending. A poorly administered re-settlement strategy for prisoners will undermine a well-thought-through policy reform.) This means that responsibility for outcomes will often be blurred.

But while we recognise that there is no pure and binary distinction between 'policy' and 'operations' we do not believe complexity should be used as an argument for inertia. The distinction between policy and operations is already employed successfully in other domains and by Whitehall itself. Broadly speaking, it not only structures relations between, say, the governing boards and executives of private companies and registered charities, or between executive local government councillors and council officers, but between Whitehall departments and their agencies.[18] International experience also points to its workability (see Box 5.3 on New Zealand).

Moreover, while the distinction is hard to make in some cases, it is often relatively clear (Polidano 1999; Barberis 1998). The recent paradigm here is perhaps provided by Gordon Brown's decision to give discretion over the setting of interest rates to the monetary committee of the Bank of England. The Treasury remains responsible for setting broad macroeconomic targets, but officials are responsible for delivering on them.

We argue, in fact, that developments over recent decades have made the distinction less hard to make than it once was; indeed, we suggest that these developments make some sort of division of responsibilities, of the kind we are advocating, very hard to resist. The role of the civil service has under-

---

Box 5.2 Building on the accounting officer principle

The Accounting Officer principle offers a well-established precedent for making a clear demarcation of civil service responsibilities of the sort that we advocate. In their capacity as departmental accounting officers, Permanent Secretaries are directly and personally accountable to Parliament – through the Public Accounts Committee – for the regularity, propriety and efficient use of public money spent by their departments. In this respect they can, but infrequently do, refuse to endorse ministerial policies that they consider to be an inefficient use of public money. If they believe that something a minister calls for is in breach of the requirements of propriety or regularity, the Permanent Secretary will set out in writing his or her objections. If ministers wish to proceed regardless, then they have to publicly issue a directive stating their intentions to do so, thus absolving the Permanent Secretary of personal responsibility and accountability.

It is extremely rare for Permanent Secretaries to use this 'nuclear option'. There are only two examples from recent memory: in 1975, Sir Peter Carey refused to endorse Tony Benn's scheme for a workers co-operative, and, in 1993, Sir Tim Lankester declined to support government policy on the Peragu Dam (Weir and Beetham, 1999).

The Accounting Officer principle demonstrates not only that it is possible to hold civil servants directly accountable, it also points the way forward for how disagreements between ministers and mandarins can be best managed and resolved.

gone a fundamental alteration since the 1980s. It is now expected not only to run ministers' offices and advise on policy but to direct services, and deliver 'outcomes' for service users and citizens. The Prime Minister put it best himself when he said: 'the principal challenge is to shift focus from policy advice to delivery' (Blair 2004).

This change, however, makes it easier to hold the service to account – to make a distinction between 'policy', the responsibility of ministers, and 'delivery' the responsibility of civil servants, and to assess, in relatively objective terms, the extent to which civil servants are meeting the objective they have agreed to try to meet (Barberis 1998). Certainly, many of the civil servants we interviewed argued that not only was there a need to strengthen accountability in the service, but also greater opportunities to do so than ever before.

> A quiet revolution is taking place in Whitehall, which the outside world and some ministers have failed to notice. The 'delivery' agenda has fundamentally changed the mechanics of Whitehall. The senior civil service is moving away from the traditional 'managing politics model' to a 'delivery model'. This is changing the role of Permanent Secretaries and challenging the traditional relationship between ministers and official. (Permanent Secretary)

> It is beyond doubt that the nineteenth-century constitutional arrangements underpinning the British civil service need examining. The changing context of government – especially the increased emphasis on delivering results – is pushing those conventions to the limit. Performance is adversely affected. (Senior official)

> There is a muddle over ministers/officials roles and responsibilities – this is beginning to bite and become and a live issue. I would agree that a quiet revolution has taken place and that ministers have not realised that the role of officials has changed significantly in recent years. You have to remember that, despite all the rhetoric about delivery, ministers still want a traditional policy advice/political management service from officials. While our roles have changed significantly, the role of ministers has hardly changed at all. (Permanent Secretary)

> Developing separate spheres of accountability would present challenges and represent a shift to the way of doing things. But these are surmountable. This is the direction we are moving in with the advent of PSAs and other initiatives. As Whitehall becomes more focused on delivery, there will be more scope for greater accountability. The infrastructure is being put in place. We just need to use it. (Permanent Secretary)

The shift to a delivery-focused model of Whitehall has served to blur the roles of ministers and civil servants. What are we here to do? If I am to be made accountable for running and managing the department effectively and for delivering outcomes then we need to ask what I am responsible for and what the minister is responsible for. Do I run the department? If I am to be held accountable for it, should I? Most ministers are uninterested in running departments; even those that think they run them, in reality don't – they simply don't have the time. (Permanent Secretary)

An erosion of democracy?

Even if the policy/operations split is a practicable one, some will advance another objection to our recommendations – that giving civil servants greater external accountability for operations, and limiting ministers' responsibility to matters of policy, would represent an unacceptable dilution of parliamentary sovereignty. We concede that, as already said, the reforms we advocate would represent a significant revision of the convention of ministerial responsibility. Ministers would no longer have even formal responsibility for every corner of the civil service.

We are not, however, persuaded that our reforms would amount to a weakening of democratic accountability in Whitehall. First, as we argued in the last chapter, current arrangements mean that, too often, no one is properly accountable. The doctrine of ministerial responsibility and other governing civil service conventions allow ministers and mandarins to duck and hide behind one another. Domains of responsibility are ill-defined, and lines of answerability hopelessly confused.

Second, the power that ministers would be delegating is, in fact, relatively limited. Most ministers take a fairly hands-off approach to departmental management.

Third, the elected government of the day would retain control in crucial respects. It would be for the government, not the civil service or its governing body, to take decisions about the shape, configuration and size of the civil service – though it could now expect the support of a governing board and executive equipped to help them in making their decisions. It would remain for government to decide, for instance, on the extent to which civil service functions should be, say, devolved to local government or local agencies, privatised, or expanded.

And ministers would continue to hold the purse strings – perhaps the most important form of control of all! Ministers could also be given the right to make operational decisions themselves on the condition that they formally acknowledge that they are relieving civil servants of their responsibilities. The model here is provided by the convention that allows ministers to overrule Permanent Secretaries when the latter are acting in their capacity as accounting officers (see Box 5.2).

Finally, it should be pointed out that, even under our proposals, Parliament would retain ultimate control of the civil service. The reforms we advocate would be introduced through an Act of Parliament, and could be altered or repealed by a further Act.

In these circumstances, concerns about loss of ministerial authority look exaggerated. Rather than seeing such reforms as an affront to democracy, it is better, we argue, to see them as an attempt to make democratic government work better. Any loss of power would, we suggest, be compensated for by a gain in civil service effectiveness. Our reforms are intended to recast ministerial-civil service relations, to get ministers and civil servants to focus on what they are good at: ministers to focus on policy, and civil servants, as a professional cadre of managers, left to manage and drive forward the government's programme.

Before turning to our recommendations, we make one final point. Throughout the last chapter and this, we have argued for the importance of improving Whitehall's accountability system – and in particular of making sure that civil servants and ministers are properly held to account. Many might think that we, therefore, want the service to become a harsher, more competitive, less trusting place to work, and will be concerned about the impact of these changes on the ethos and, ultimately, effectiveness of the service itself. On the contrary, we recognise the dangers inherent in overly narrow and heavy-handed performance regimes. We merely contend that not every performance regime needs to be narrow and heavy-handed. We suggest, indeed, that a clearer demarcation of responsibilities could help dispel the mistrust with perhaps increasingly discolours relations between ministers and mandarins.

Below we lay out our recommendations in more detail.

Performance and accountability in Whitehall: recommendations

1. Creation of a Civil Service Board of Governors

We recommend the creation of a new governing body for the civil service. This body would have three core functions:

- Setting the vision for the civil service and defining its role and purpose. As we suggested in Chapter 2, the values and role of the civil service need to change with the times. The Civil Service Governors would be charged with defining and re-defining its values and role. The government of the day should retain ultimate responsibility for decisions over the basic size and shape of the service, and the role of private, voluntary and local agencies in delivering outcomes. These are political matters.

But the governing board should assist the government in developing its civil service policies, overseeing their realisation, and ensuring that the service remains a neutral, open, outward-looking and effective service, focused on serving citizens and service users. We do not believe that these functions would be effectively performed by the new Civil Service Executive, which will be preoccupied with more day to day duties.[19]

- Appointing a civil service chief executive – the Head of the Civil Service – and managing his or her performance. (For the Head of the Civil Service and the Civil Service Executive, see recommendation 2.) We do not believe that it would be satisfactory for the Prime Minister to appoint the Head of the Civil Service, because this might compromise civil service neutrality, and muddy the clearer demarcation between policy and operations that we favour. The Prime Minister, however, should be given the power to veto nominations put forward by the governors.

- Laying down what is expected of mandarins and ministers both by way of 'ethical' conduct and good practice. The board would thus take over the role of Civil Service Commissioners, whose job it is to hear cases of possible abuse of the Civil Service Code. But, it would go beyond the Commissioner's remit, in promoting professional or best-practice standards on the part of ministers and mandarins. Civil Service Governors would similarly be responsible for helping ministers and officials in drawing distinctions between policy and operational matters. They would also be charged with regulating the distinction – that is, investigating cases of administrative failure and, where required, laying out, as far as possible, where responsibility for the failure lies.

Civil Service Governors should be appointed by Parliament, though appointments should have to be approved by the Prime Minister. We strongly recommend that the members of the board should be drawn from a range of backgrounds – from Whitehall itself, and from Parliament, local government and the voluntary and private sectors.

2. Creation of a Civil Service Executive

We recommend the creation of a centralised and impartial Civil Service Executive – modelled loosely on the New Zealand State Service Commission (see Box 5.3) – led by an empowered Head of the Civil Service, who would be responsible for the day-to-day direction of the civil service. The executive would be tasked with giving the civil service the strong corporate centre it badly needs.

The Head of the Civil Service would be supported by a number of deputy directors, each assigned an area of executive responsibility. These might include:

- recruitment, remuneration and performance accountability

- training and skills development
- ICT and knowledge management
- financial management
- communications
- public attitudes and public engagement
- sustainability, design and estate management
- policy development
- public services improvement.

We recommend that the posts of Cabinet Secretary and Head of the Civil Service be split. The current role of the Cabinet Secretary would be handled by the new Permanent Secretary of the Department for the Prime Minister and Cabinet (see recommendation 7 below).

Roles and functions
The core functions of the Civil Service Executive would be to:

- Lead the senior civil service as a corporate entity and manage civil service-wide processes
- Appoint, employ and line-manage Permanent Secretaries
- Evaluate and oversee the performance of government departments and Permanent Secretaries on behalf of their Secretaries of State, with the power to remove poor performers and reward high performers
- Support the Civil Service Governors, Prime Minister and other ministers in setting the service's strategic direction
- Work with ministers, Treasury officials, Permanent Secretaries and their senior officers to set departmental strategies and targets – including cross-cutting or inter-departmental strategies and targets
- Ensure that Whitehall has the capacity and capabilities to deliver the government of the day's programme, including promoting and developing the senior leadership and management capability of the service.

The civil service Head should be appointed by the new Civil Service Board of Governors on a fixed but renewable five-year contract. The Prime Minister would be able to reject a name put forward by the governors.

The Head of the Civil Service should be responsible for appointing and line-managing deputy directors. Executive posts should be publicly advertised, with the aim of ensuring a balance of career civil servants and outsiders among senior executives.

Holding the Head of the Civil Service to account
The Head of the Civil Service should be formally accountable to the Civil Service Governors. The Prime Minister and ministers will be asked to feed in their views on the performance of the Head of the Civil Service during

his/her annual review. She or he would also be made accountable to Parliament in her or his capacity as accounting officer for the Civil Service Executive and for delivering its core objectives. The civil service Head should have to submit an annual report to Parliament, and be subject to an annual session before Parliament, allowing MPs to scrutinise the performance of the Executive and the civil service overall.

The Civil Service Executive and its relationship with ministers

- **Appointment:** The Head of the Civil Service should be responsible for appointing Permanent Secretaries. We recommend that ministers be given an opportunity, at the outset of the process, to specify the qualities and skills they think most important in the new appointee. The civil service Head should present the Prime Minister and departmental minister with a name. The Prime Minister and departmental minister should also have the power of veto over any name put forward by the Head of the Civil Service and ask him or her to hold another round of interviews. As in New Zealand, ministers should be allowed to make a unilateral appointment, but such a move should have to be accompanied by a public declaration to Parliament stating the reasons behind the decision. This acts as a strong deterrent against this course of action.
- **Transparency:** We also recommend that the Civil Service Executive overhaul the current arrangements for appointing Permanent Secretaries, which lack transparency. Permanent secretaries will be appointed for five-year fixed-term renewable contracts. All vacancies will be automatically subject to open competition and advertised externally.
- **Performance accountability:** Drawing on its own assessment of Permanent Secretary performance, and external assessments (see below), the Head of the Civil Service will have the power to remove poor performers and reward strong performers. The Head of the Civil Service should involve ministers closely in appraising and managing their Permanent Secretaries. To ensure that the Head of the Civil Service is kept regularly informed about Permanent Secretary and departmental performance, he or she will appoint non-executive directors to sit on departmental boards. In the case of a serious problem, the Head of the Civil Service will be able to remove Permanent Secretaries within their contracts.

3. A new role for Permanent Secretaries

We recommend that Permanent Secretaries should become personally accountable for all department operations, including decisions over recruitment and promotion and remuneration. Permanent Secretaries would be answerable to the Head of the Civil Service for their performance, and ultimately to the Civil Service Governors and Parliament. They would also be expected to represent the department to the media and the pubic for those matters delegated to them. Permanent Secretaries would continue to work closely with ministers in developing policy, and managing departmental and parliamentary business – though ministers should be able to draw on a wider range of advisers and other sources for policy advice (see recommendation 5).

Box 5.3 The case of New Zealand

Respective roles of ministers and chief executives
In New Zealand the respective roles of ministers and chief executives (Permanent Secretary equivalents) are defined in statute.

- Ministers are politically accountable to parliament (and the public) for the conduct of their agencies – they are responsible for strategic direction, policy decisions, the public advocacy of the decisions made, and 'outcomes'.
- Chief executives are responsible to their ministers for the conduct of their agencies – they are responsible for policy advice and implementation, service delivery, the management of their agencies, 'outputs' and 'managing for outcomes'.

Accountability in New Zealand
New Zealand undertook radical and large-scale reforms to its public sector and civil service in the 1980s. At the heart of the reforms was a desire to improve the accountability of the public service by establishing clear lines of responsibility between ministers and civil servants and instilling a new sense of personal accountability in the latter.

The architects of New Zealand's management reforms envisioned ministers and chief executives in a contractualised principal-agent relationship in which ministers would 'purchase' outputs from chief executives using a system of detailed purchase agreements. However, this arrangement proved problematic as it was costly and rigid, and ministers proved to be largely uninterested in negotiating contracts. The system evolved so that the State Service Commission became the principle assessor of chief executive performance, with ministers providing valuable feedback. Detailed purchase agreements have been replaced with more streamlined and outcome focused Statements of Intent and Output Plans, which set out ministerial objectives, and civil service delivery plans.

A 2001 government review of the reforms declared that one of their greatest successes was that 'accountability is taken seriously in the system' (Review of the Centre 2001).

cont. next page

The role of chief executives

The unified career civil service that it inherited from Britain was effectively abolished as permanent department heads were replaced with chief executives, appointed via open competition on fixed-term contracts. Unlike permanent heads, chief executives are personally accountable for all department operations, including the management of its staff, and have the freedom to make all input decisions, including pay, staffing, organisation structure, and service delivery. Chief executives oversee the hiring and firing of staff, respond to parliamentary committees, and represent the department to the media and public for those matters delegated to them. Initially, chief executives were only responsible for departmental outputs, but now they are also responsible for 'managing outcomes', which requires them to take a broader view of their work and its impact on government policy as a whole, and encourages collaboration with new actors.

The role of ministers

Ministers are accountable to Parliament for departmental outcomes. They are rarely drawn into the day-to-day operations of departments. Instead, their role is to develop strategic objectives and policies and to 'steer' government departments by providing them with resources, helping them to develop departmental Statements of Intent and monitoring their Output Plans. They are collectively responsible for the overall capacity of government.

Accountability mechanisms

Chief executives are accountable to Parliament for the financial management and financial performance of their department. As part of the annual budget round, chief executives must prepare a Statement of Intent for their minister to have tabled in Parliament, which provides a base against which the department's actual performance is later assessed. This Statement must be followed up with an Output Plan, a more detailed work programme that will deliver on these priorities. Both the Statement of Intent and the Output Plan are scrutinised annually by the relevant parliamentary select committee, which uses these documents to formally evaluate the department in the form of a Financial Review. This Review evaluates the success of the department's annual undertakings in a clear and accessible manner, and incorporates financial and service performance ratings from the Auditor-General.

The State Services Commissioner assesses chief executive performance annually. If it is unsatisfactory, he or she can decide not to renew the chief executive's contract. The Commissioner has the power, with the approval of the Cabinet, to dismiss a chief executive.

If civil servants consider that their minister is seeking to exert too much influence over matters that are properly within the domain of the chief executive they can raise their concerns with the chief executive, who should attempt to clarify and resolve any concern by discussion with the minister. If concern remains the chief executive will record in writing (for example, by seeking written directions from the minister or recording the decision/view as conveyed by the minister). If necessary, the opinion of the State Service Commission will be sought (see www.ssc.govt.nz).

4. A new role for ministers

We recommend that ministers should not longer be responsible for day-to-day operations – unless, that is, they expressly take on responsibility for a particular project or other operational area. At the same time, ministers should be held properly to account for matters over which they remain responsible – especially policy. Where conflict and disagreement arise, the issue would be referred for adjudication to the Civil Service Executive or, ultimately, the Civil Service Governors and Parliament.

We hope and believe that encouraging ministers to concentrate on policy will promote better policymaking in Whitehall. For one thing, it should allow ministers and their advisers to concentrate more fully on policy assessment and development. We also believe that it will facilitate a much needed opening up of the policymaking process. As things work now, Whitehall, unsure of its responsibilities and prerogatives, tends to look warily on external advisers and policy experts. We suggest that clearer demarcation of roles and a better system of holding civil servants and ministers to account, will help allay its concerns.

We recommend, in particular, that ministers should be able to set up *cabinet* systems to help them in their more limited policy roles, and see the council of economic advisers at HM Treasury as a model to follow. The use of special advisers has caused great controversy, but we believe that they have a positive contribution to make. 'Politicisation' did not, in fact, emerge as a major concern among the civil servants and others we interviewed. Most Permanent Secretaries seem to see special advisers in a fairly positive light.

Nevertheless, in recommending cabinet systems we recognise the need to ensure that the principles of transparency and accountability we propose for civil servants should also apply to advisers working in these cabinets.

Parliament should be allowed to call any cabinet adviser before them. Members of cabinets should, moreover, remain advisers. They should not be given formal power to direct civil servants.

5. Civil service careers: ending permanence and increasing accountability

We recommend the further opening up of Whitehall's career structure and ending the principle, still largely observed, that a job in the civil service is a job for life. All senior civil service appointments should be subject to open competition and be publicly advertised. Officials should be appointed to posts for fixed lengths of time, renewable subject to contract, and public servants should expect to move in and out of the service through their careers. This will increase the gene pool of talent available to Permanent Secretaries when making appointments. It will contribute to clear lines of accountability, which, we have argued, the service badly needs. Finally, it would help break down the suspicion of 'outsiders' that, we have seen, still exists in Whitehall.

However, though posts would be time-limited and appointed to a specific job rather than to a grade, the time of posts should be extended. This would address a major concern that was continually raised with us: that civil servants moved around far too much.

6. Ending Whitehall exceptionalism: external performance assessment for Whitehall

We recommend that the Civil Service Governors, in partnership with Parliament, commission a regular independent assessment of civil service departments, agencies and the Civil Service Executive. While central government believes that public agencies should be subject to independent scrutiny, and has imposed countless assessment regimes on others, it has managed to escape subjection itself. Whitehall should no longer continue to mark its own exams. Only a regular, externally validated assessment of departmental performance will allow departments to build on their strengths and address their weaknesses. Without such assessment, it will be near impossible for Civil Service Governors and Parliament to hold mandarins and ministers to proper account. We therefore recommend that Departmental Capability Reviews be conducted externally.

7. A new relationship with Parliament: towards 'whole of government' accountability

We do not believe that Parliament alone can do the job of governing the civil service or holding it to account. The civil service needs a body dedicated exclusively to elaborating a vision for the service, developing a long-term strategy and scrutinising performance. This is why we have recommended the creation of a Civil Service Board of Governors. Nevertheless, we believe that Parliament and its Select Committees should continue to play an important role in scrutinising the Civil Service. Indeed, one important effect of the reforms advocated here would be to give Parliament and its committees a new role in holding not just ministers but civil servants to account. Against this background we recommend that:

- Select committees continue to scrutinise departmental performance, but also begin to scrutinise the performance of civil servants with formal operational responsibilities.
- The rules and conventions protecting civil servants from parliamentary scrutiny be reformed. Parliament must be able to effectively effectively hold the civil service to account for those areas for which it has been given operational responsibility. Protection would remain in place for the scrutiny of policy.
- Select committees be given a mechanism for reporting a loss of confidence in a part of the civil service or civil servant, following their inquiries, to the Civil Service Governors. The Governors and the Executive should incorporate these views in their assessment of departmental performance.
- All relevant information concerning the detailed responsibilities of senior civil servants (Director General and above) should be made available to the relevant select committee. A list of ministerial responsibilities is regularly published – an equivalent is needed for senior civil servants.[20] Civil service performance agreements – those that underpin PSA objectives – should also be published. An accountable civil service can no longer be an anonymous and invisible civil service.

8. A new department for the Prime Minister and the Cabinet

We recommend splitting the posts of Head of the Civil Service and Cabinet Secretary, and the creation of a Department for the Prime Minister and Cabinet, with the Cabinet Secretary becoming, in effect, the Permanent Secretary of the new department. This department would be responsible for running the Prime Minister's Office, and serving the Cabinet and cabinet committees. The Department for the Prime Minister and Cabinet would naturally take on a special responsibility for government policy and policy development, and would work closely with the deputy director responsible for policy development.

Despite formal separation of the posts of Head of Civil Service and Cabinet Secretary, we would expect a close working relationship between Executive and Cabinet Office and Prime Minister. Indeed, we recommend that the Head of the Civil Service attend Cabinet alongside the Cabinet Secretary.

9. A Civil Service Act

We recommend that our proposals be enshrined in a Civil Service Act. This would:

- set out the principles governing the new relationship between ministers and officials (and special advisers)

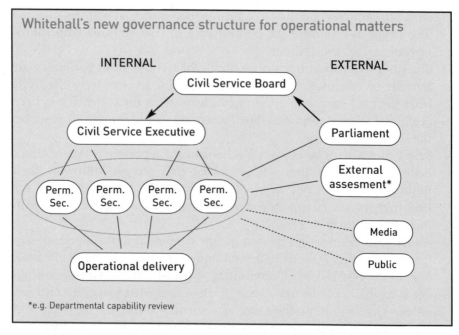

Whitehall's new governance structure for operational matters

INTERNAL   EXTERNAL

Civil Service Board

Civil Service Executive   Parliament

Perm. Sec.   Perm. Sec.   Perm. Sec.   Perm. Sec.   External assesment*

Media

Operational delivery   Public

*e.g. Departmental capability review

- broadly define the respective roles and responsibilities of ministers and officials
- define the powers of Civil Service Board of Governors, Civil Service Executive, Ministers, Permanent Secretaries and Parliament (and its committees)
- determine procedures for the resolution of any disputes over the division of responsibilities between ministers and civil servants.

The Act would also, explicitly or implicitly, put an end to the conventions and rules – including the Osmotherly rules – guarding the anonymity of civil servants, at least in cases where they have been given full operational responsibility. They would remain in place for scrutiny of policy.

We believe that it is vitally important that Parliament give formal recognition to the recasting of the doctrine of ministerial responsibility and the division of responsibilities between ministers and Whitehall that we are advocating. The traditional doctrine of ministerial responsibility, though vague and contested, remains powerful and it will be very difficult to establish new, clearer lines of accountability, unless ministerial responsibility is reformulated in statute.

Box 5.4 Forging a new division of responsibilities: a concordat between ministers and officials

As a first step to creating the new civil service governance structure and Civil Service Act for which we argue, we recommend the establishment of a concordat between ministers, the civil service and Parliament. As a forerunner to a Civil Service Act, this would:

- broadly define the respective roles and responsibilities of ministers and officials, and the areas where accountability and responsibility will be delegated to civil servants
- determine the resolution procedures needed to deal with any disputes over the division of responsibilities
- define the powers of Parliament (and its committees) in relation to the operation of the division of responsibilities between ministers and Parliament.

The concordat would then be piloted to test the workability of the policy operations distinction in relation to central government and the effectiveness of the new accountability arrangements.

6 Conclusion: Making the case for Whitehall reform

We have argued that most of Whitehall's problems can be traced to the inadequacies in the way it is governed. If it finds it difficult to adapt and innovate, to achieve the highest standards of professionalism and expertise, to work across boundaries, to learn lessons, look outwards, this is in large part because responsibility for performance and management are poorly defined.

We have also argued that these problems cannot be fixed by another wave or managerial reforms, focused, say, on getting in new blood, improving training, imposing more targets, or re-organising departments. We need to get to the roots of Whitehall's weaknesses and reform the way it is directed, and held to account.

This might sound like a daunting task. We want to stress, therefore, by way of conclusion, that we believe that opportunity for radical reform is there for the taking. The prospects for the civil service are, perhaps, better than they have been for many generations.

As we have said, a number of factors, including successive reforms, from the Fulton reforms of the 1960s, through the Next Steps programme of the 1980s and 90s to the introduction of explicit departmental targets more recently, have worked to increase the independence of individual civil servants, many of whom now have de facto responsibility for particular spheres of work. Giving civil servants formal responsibility would merely recognise this change and ensure that they were properly held to account.

At the same time, both civil servants and politicians seem increasingly to acknowledge the need to clarify the terms of exchange between them and lay out a clearer demarcation of responsibilities. And all agree on the need to strengthen Whitehall's capacity for strategic thinking, leadership and innovation. The challenge before civil servants, and, above all, politicians then, is to exploit the opportunity and appetite for change before them. Most of the public might not care very much about civil service reform. But they care about prosperity, public services, security and sustainability – and effective management of these things depends on an effective civil service. The time has come to reform the way Whitehall and relations between Whitehall and ministers are governed.

Endnotes

1. The debacle at the Home Office over the release of foreign prisoners in May 2006 coincided with a series of administrative problems across Whitehall (including at the Department for the Environment, Rural Affairs and Food, the Department of Health and HM Revenue and Customs).
2. Fortunately, however, there are some exceptions – with regard to middle-ranking civil servants, see Page and Jenkins (2005), and for work on agencies see Talbot (2004).
3. In fact, the history of Whitehall is littered with examples of politicisation. Iain Mclean has shown that Sir George Murray, Permanent Secretary at the Treasury while Lloyd George was Chancellor, would regularly write to Lloyd George's sworn political enemy Lord Rosebery, encouraging him to block his budgets (cited in O'Donnell 2005). More recently, Hennessy (2001) has argued that William Armstrong, head of the civil service under Edward Heath, had become too closely identified with the Prime Minister and would probably have resigned when Labour came to power in 1974, had he not left due to ill health.
4. It is revealing that reform programmes characteristically avoid articulating any particular view of what role Whitehall should play. The recent Gershon review was typical in this respect. Though processes set in train by the review are, in effect, reshaping the civil service, the review itself started with the question 'how much government do we need?', rather than 'what kind of government do we need?'
5. As our report went to print the first tranches of Departmental Capability Reviews were published. These exposed some major shortcomings with the four departments that were assessed (the Home Office, Department for Constitutional Affairs, Department of Work and Pensions and the Department for Education and Skills), especially relating to leadership and delivery capabilities. Many of the findings agree with our conclusions.
6. Indeed, it has been said that the 'great flaw' of the Northcote-Trevelyan report (see Chapter 2) was its insistence that it was 'better to train young men' than it was to 'take men of mature age' into the service (Hennessy 2001). The exceptions to this practice were provided by the two world wars, when Whitehall opened itself up to outside influences and expertise (ibid).
7. Our figures are calculated by focusing specifically on the Whitehall village – the departments represented in Table 3.1, whereas the full SCS staff survey covers the whole SCS, including agencies and other departments. For the full SCS, the figures are as follows: policy 50; corporate services 16; and operational delivery 34 (Cabinet Office 2005).

8. These figures have been calculated by using membership of the Permanent Secretaries Management Group (PSMG) as of 19 December 2005. Just one 'outsider' sits on the Permanent Secretaries' Steering Group, which is a more active group than the PSMG.

9. Reflecting this, the influential Public Administration Select Committee has launched an inquiry into *Governing the Future*, with the aim of exploring how the civil service can improve the effectiveness of its strategic and long-term thinking in government (PASC 2005).

10. In fact, this is not only the picture in Britain; it appears much the same in many other OECD countries (OECD 2001). It is just more surprising, given its permanence. Some international case studies offer examples of best practice: the Danish government has pioneered the use of 'intellectual capital statements', which report on an organisation's knowledge management activities, and help to identify knowledge resources. The US Navy is renowned for the importance it attaches to institutional memory.

11. Even Baroness Usha Prashar, first civil service commissioner, has acknowledged this point: 'The civil service, possibly more than any other institution, has had little guidance as an organisation to shape its development. Since the demise of the Royal Institute of Public Administration there has not been an independent forum for discussion about the civil service. Reforms, particularly since the 1980s, have been driven in response to external pressures, perceived dilemmas and political drivers, rather than any continuous systematic assessment of the organisation. The agenda for reform has been predominantly managerial, and much of it has been implemented without much engagement of the public or parliament' (Prashar n.d.: 11).

12. Performance Partnership Agreements (PPAs) were the forerunner to the Departmental Capability Reviews. Established by Sir Andrew Turnbull, they were a form of performance contract between the Cabinet Secretary and departmental permanent secretaries.

13. To put this into perspective, we compared this figure with that held by a 'major professional service organisation' in the private sector. In a similar staff survey, 40 per cent of staff felt that poor performance was adequately dealt with. They also told us that they were not satisfied with this figure and wanted it to rise to 60 per cent.

14. An important exception to Whitehall non-accountability comes in the form of the accounting officer principle (see Chapter 5).

15. Though, even in this period, commentators were sceptical about the usefulness of ministerial responsibility. Writing in 1920, Sidney and Beatrice Webb argued that it was 'illusory as an instrument of democratic control' (quoted in Barberis 1998).

16. This problem has long been recognised – see, for example, Hennessy (2001) quoting William Ryrie's evidence to the Fulton Committee, 1968, as well as the Home Office report *From Improvement to Transformation* (Home Office

2006) for a recent statement.

17. The Fulton and Next Steps reforms – the most radical attempts to transform the civil service in the post-war period – clearly illustrate this. In devising the terms of reference for the Fulton Committee, Harold Wilson, a strong advocate of civil service reform, deliberately ruled out any change to the relationship between ministers and civil servants (Hennessy 2001). Meanwhile, the Thatcher government rejected a central recommendation of the Next Steps report, which was that the managerial changes it advocated should be accompanied by a change to the doctrine of ministerial responsibility (Cabinet Office 1988).

18. The Next Steps reforms undoubtedly encountered some initial teething problems, especially in the case of the Prisons Agency and the Child Support Agency, but on the whole they are deemed to have implemented a workable distinction between policy and operations (Greer 1994, 1995; Mountfield 1997; Polidano 1997). The Next Steps reforms also provide a valuable lesson for the future. The decision not to amend the accountability framework – and to leave ministerial responsibility in place and hence blur the relationship between ministers and agency executives – meant that the agency reforms have had less impact than they should have (Davies and Williams, 1991; ippr interviews). Since ministers remain responsible they are able to intervene as and when they like; instead of looking outwards, most agencies look upwards to the parent departments. We argue that the Next Steps reforms were limited in their impact because they were limited in their scope: managerial reforms, to succeed, need to be aligned with changes to the constitutional make-up.

19. It would be a mistake to overburden one body with strategic and executive functions. Certainly this was the experience of the New Zealand State Service Commission, which struggled to provide strategic leadership of the sort we are looking to the civil service governors to provide, since it was also simultaneously responsible for a range of important executive functions (Norman 2003).

20. Some departments publish the responsibilities of board-level officials. Some even say which officials are responsible for delivery of specific PSAs. But much could be done to improve this.

References

Adams J and Schmuecker K (2005) *Devolution in Practice 2006* London: Institute for Public Policy Research

Almond G and Verba S (1989) *The Civic Culture: Political Attitudes and Democracy in Five Nations* London: Sage

Aucoin P (2006) 'The Staffing and Evaluation of Canadian Deputy Ministers in Comparative Westminster Perspective: A Proposal for Reform' *Restoring Accountability Research Studies Volume 1, Commission of Inquiry into the Sponsorship Program and Advertising Activities* Ottawa: Gomery Commission

Audit Commission (2005) *CPA – The Harder Test: Scores and analysis of performance in single tier and county councils 2005* London: Audit Commission

Bagehot W (2001) *The English Constitution* Oxford: OUP

Balogh T (1959) 'The Apotheosis of the Dilettante' in Thomas H *The Establishment* London: Anthony Blond

Barberis P (1998) 'The New Public Management and a New Accountability' in *Public Administration* 36 Autumn: 451-470

Barnett C (1986) *The Audit of War: The Illusion & Reality of Britain as a Great Nation* Basingstoke: Macmillan

Bichard M (1999) *Performance Management Civil Service Reform – A Report to the Meeting of Permanent Heads of Departments, Sunningdale 30 September – 1 October 1999* London: HMSO

Bichard M (2004) 'Mission-driven government' in Byrne L and Collins P *Reinventing Government Again* London: Social Market Foundation

Bichard M (2005) 'Is public service reform delivering?' Audit Commission inaugural Annual Lecture and Debate, Wednesday 13 July

Bichard M (2006) 'The profession for public service' in Craig J (ed) *Production Values: Futures for Professionalism* London: Demos

Blair T (1998) 'Speech on the Civil Service' Civil Service Conference Speech, 13 October, available from www.number10.gov.uk

Blair T (2004) 'Speech on Civil Service Reform' Speech at the Civil Service Reform, Delivery and Values event, 24 February, available at www.number10.gov.uk

Blunkett D (2006) *Memorandum by Rt Hon David Blunkett MP to the Public Administration Select Committee* Politics and Administration: Ministers and Civil Servants Inquiry, 29 June

Bogdanor V (2001) 'Civil Service Reform: A Critique' in *Political Quarterly* Vol 72 Issue 3, July

Bogdanor V (2003) 'The Civil Service' in Bogdanor V (ed) *The British Constitution in the Twentieth Century* Oxford: British Academy/OUP

Bogdanor V (2005) 'Introduction' in Bogdanor V (ed) *Joined-Up Government* Oxford: Oxford University Press

Boston J and Eichbaum C (2005) *State Sector Reform and Renewal in New Zealand: Lessons for Governance,* Paper prepared for Conference on 'Repositioning of Public Governance – Global Experiences and Challenges' Taipei, 18-19 November 2005

Cabinet Office (1988) *Improving Management in Government: The Next Steps* London: HMSO

Cabinet Office (1996) *The Civil Service Code* London: HMSO

Cabinet Office (1999) *The Civil Service Code* London: HMSO

Cabinet Office (2001) *Better Policy Making* London: HMSO

Cabinet Office (2005) *Report for Senior Civil Service: Overall Senior Civil Service Leadership and Skill Survey 2004* Internal Benchmarking Report, London: HMSO

Cabinet Office (2006) *The Civil Service Code* London: HMSO

Cabinet Office/ippr (forthcoming) *Senior Civil Service Leadership and Skills Survey by Department* (obtained by ippr under FOI, due to be published. Available from www.ippr.org)

Chapman R (1988) *Ethics in the British Civil Service* London: Routledge

Chapman J (2002) *System Failure: Why governments must learn to think differently* London: Demos

Civil Service Commissioners (2005) *Changing Times: Leading Perspectives on the Civil Service in the 21st century and its enduring values* London: The Office of the Civil Service Commissioners

Civil Service Commissioners (2006) *Annual Report 2005-06 Supporting an effective and impartial civil service* London: HMSO

Clarke R (2002) *New Democratic Processes: better decisions, stronger democracy* London: Institute for Public Policy Research

Cornforth C (2003) *The Governance of Public and Non-Profit Organizations: What Boards do* London: Routledge

Crossman R (1975) *The Diaries of a Cabinet Minister* London: Hamilton and Cape

Davies A and Williams J (1991) *What Next? Agencies, Departments and the Civil Service* London: Institute for Public Policy Research

Darwell R (2006) *The Reluctant Managers: Reforming Whitehall* London: KPMG

Department of Health (2006) *Our Health, Our Care, Our Say* London: The Stationery Office

Donahue J and Nye J (2003) *For the People: Can We Fix Public Service?* Washington DC: Brookings Institute

Dowding K (1995) *The Civil Service* London: Routledge

Drewry G (2004) 'The Executive: Towards Accountable Government and Effective Governance' in Jowell J and Oliver D (eds) *The Changing Constitution* Fifth Edition, Oxford: OUP

Dynes M and Walker D (1995) *The New British State* London: Times Book

Fabian Society (1967) *The Administrators* London: Fabian Society

Flinders M (2005) *MPs and Icebergs: Parliament and Delegated Governance* Paper presented to the 2005 PSA conference

Foster C (2005a) 'Joined Up Government and Cabinet Government' in Bogdanor V (ed) *Joined Up Government* Oxford: British Academy/OUP

Foster C (2005b) *A Crisis in British Government* London: Hart

Fraser, Lord (2004) *A Report by the Rt Hon Lord Fraser of Carmyllie QC on the Holyrood Inquiry* Edinburgh: The Stationery Office

Fry GK (1970) 'The Sachsenhausen Concentration Camp Case and the Convention of Ministerial Responsibility' in *Public Law* Winter: 336-357

Fulton Committee (1968) *The Civil Service, Report of the Committee Vol.1* London: HMSO

Gay O (2005) *The Osmotherly Rules* House of Commons Library Standard Note SN/PC/2671, 4 August

Goldsmith S and Eggers WD (2004) *Governing by Network: The New Shape of the Public Sector* Washington DC: Brookings Institution Press

Goss S (2005) 'The reform of public service reform' in *Renewal* Vol 13 2/3

Goss S (forthcoming 2006) 'Re-inventing the public realm' in Hassan G (ed) *After Blair* London: Lawrence and Wishart

Greer P (1994) *Transforming Central Government: The Next Step Initiative* Buckingham: OUP

Greer P (1995) *The Department of Social Security and its Agencies* Basingstoke: Macmillan

Hartley J (2005) 'Innovation in Governance and Public Services: Past and Present' in *Public Money and Management* Vol 21 No 1 January

Heclo H and Wildavsky A (1981) *The Private Government of Public Money* London: Macmillan

Hennessy P (2001) *Whitehall* London: Pimlico

HM Treasury (2005) *Corporate governance in central government departments: Code of Good Practice* London: HMSO

HM Treasury/Public Services Productivity Panel (2002) *Accountability for Results* London: HMSO

Home Office (2006) *From Improvement to Transformation* London: The Stationery Office

Hood C (2005) 'The Idea of Joined-Up Government: A Historical Perspective' in Bogdanor V (ed) *Joined Up Government* Oxford: British Academy/OUP

Hunt T (2001) *Remodelling Whitehall* London: ippr

Jay D (1947) *The Socialist Case* London: Faber and Faber

Jenkins K (2004) 'Parliament, Government and the Civil Service' in *Parliamentary Affairs* Vol. 57: 800-813, Oxford: OUP

Johnson C and Talbot C (2006) *The UK Parliament and Performance: Challenging or Challenged* Unpublished paper presented to the National Audit Office

Karmarck E (2003) 'Public Servants for Twenty-First-Century-Government' in Donahue J and Nye J (ed) *For the People: Can We Fix Public Service* Washington DC: Brookings Institute

Kaufman D, Kraay A and Mastruzzi M (2005) *Governance Matters IV: Governance Indicators for 1996-2004* Washington: World Bank

Kelly G and Muers S (2004) *Creating Public Value* London: HMSO

Labour Party (2005) 'Britain: forward not back' *The Labour Party Manifesto 2005* London: Labour Party

Leadbeater C (2002) *Innovate from Within: An Open Letter to the Cabinet Secretary* London: Demos

Levitt R and Solesbury W (2005) *Working Paper 23 Evidence-Informed Policy: What Difference do Outsiders in Whitehall Make?* Swindon: ESRC

Lind M (2005) 'In defence of mandarins' in *Prospect* October 2005, Vol. 115

Lupson J Partington D (2005) *Accountability for Public Sector IT projects and the Senior Responsible Owner: A Theoretical Background and Research Agenda* The Cranfield School of Management Working Paper Series SWP 03/05

Marquand D (2004) *Decline of the Public: The Hollowing Out of Citizenship* Cambridge: Polity Press

Marshall G (1989) *Ministerial Responsibility* Oxford: OUP

Marsh D, Richards D and Smith M (2001) *Changing Patterns of Governance in the United Kingdom: Reinventing Whitehall* Basingstoke: Palgrave

Moore M (1995) *Creating Public Value: Strategic Management in Government* Cambridge: Harvard University Press

Mountfield R (1997) 'Organisational Reform within Government: Accountability and Policy Management' in *Public Administration and Development* Vol. 17: 71-76

Mulgan G (2005a) 'Joined-Up Government: Past, Present and Future' in Bogdanor V (ed) *Joined Up Government* Oxford: OUP

Mulgan G (2005b) 'Lessons of Power' in *Prospect* May 2005

National Audit Office (2006) *Home Office: 2004-05 Resource Account* London: HMSO

Northcote S and Trevelyan C (1854) *Report on the Organisation of the Permanent Civil Service* London: HMSO

Norman R (2003) *Obedient Servants? Management Freedoms & Accountabilities in the New Zealand Public Sector* Victoria: Victoria University Press

O'Donnell G (2005) 'The Relationship between the Economy and the State' in *Changing Times: Leading Perspectives on the Civil Service in the 21st century and its enduring values* London: The Office of the Civil Service Commissioners

O'Donnell G (2006) 'The Modern Civil Service: The Fusion of Historic Values with 21st Century Dynamism' *Guardian Public Services Summit Speech* 27 January 2006, St Albans

O'Neill O (2002) *A Question of Trust* Cambridge: Cambridge University Press

OECD (2001) *Knowledge Management: Learning by Comparing Experiences from*

Private Firms and Public Organisations Summary Record of the High Level Forum, Copenhagen 8-9 February, Paris: OECD

Office of Public Service Reform (2002) *Better Government Services: Executive Agencies in the 21st century* London: HMSO

Oliver D (2003) *Constitutional Reform in the UK* Oxford: OUP

Osborne D and Gaebler T (1992) *Reinventing Government: How the Entrepreneurial Spirit is Transforming the Public Sector* Addison-Wesley

Page E and Jenkins B (2005) *Policy Bureaucracy: Government with a Cast of Thousands* Oxford: OUP

PASC (2005) *Governing the Future: An Issues and Questions Paper* London: Public Administration Select Committee

Pellow J (1982) *The Home Office 1848-1914* London

Perri 6 (2005) 'Joined up Government in the West beyond Britain: A Provisional Assessment' in Bogdanor V (ed) *Joined Up Government* Oxford: British Academy/OUP

Peters BG (2001) Future of Governing: Four Emerging Models Kansas: University of Kansas Press

Phillips H (2005) 'Why on Earth would you want to join the Civil Service in the 21st Century?' in *Changing Times: Leading Perspectives on the Civil Service in the 21st century and its enduring values* London: The Office of the Civil Service Commissioners

Pierre J and Peters BG (2000) *Governance, politics and the state* London: Macmillan

Plowden W (1994) *Ministers and Mandarins* London: ippr

Polidano C (1999) 'The Bureaucrat Who Fell Under a Bus: Ministerial responsibility, executive agencies and the Derek Lewis affair' in *Governance* Vol 12 Issue 2

Ponting C (1986) *Whitehall: Tragedy & Farce* London: Hamish Hamilton

Popper K (1945) *The Open Society and its Enemies* 2 volumes, London: Routledge and Kegan Paul

Prasher U (n.d.) 'Introduction' in Office of Civil Service Commissioners (n.d.) *Changing Times* London: Office of Civil Service Commissioners

Public magazine (2006) 'The Crack on the Edge of Whitehall' in *Public* June , London: Guardian

Public Service Committee (1996) *Ministerial Accountability and Responsibility* 1995-6 HC 313

Review of the Centre (2001) *Report of the Advisory Group on the Review of the Centre Presented to the Ministers of State Services and Finance*, Wellington: State Services Commission, November

Rhodes RAW (2000) 'New Labour's Civil Service: Summing Up Joining-Up' in *Political Quarterly* Vol 71 Issue 2, April

Rhodes RAW (2005) 'Everyday Life in a Ministry: Public Administration as Anthropology' *American Review of Public Administration* Vol. 35 No. 1: 1-23

Savoie D (1994) *Thatcher, Reagan and Mulroney: In Search of a New Bureaucracy*

Pittsburgh: University of Pittsburgh Press

Savoie D (2005) 'From Quiet Village Life to a World only for the Brave' in *Changing Times: Leading Perspectives on the Civil Service in the 21st century and its enduring values* London: The Office of the Civil Service Commissioners

Seddon J (2003) *Freedom from Command and Control* London: Vanguard Press

Smith D (2006) 'Clarifying the doctrine of Ministerial Responsibility as it applies to the Government and Parliament of Canada' in *Restoring Accountability Research Studies, Volume 1, Commission of Inquiry into the Sponsorship Program and Advertising Activities*

Smith M (1999) *The Core Executive in Britain* Basingstoke: Macmillan

SOLACE (2006) *Leadership United Final Report of the Solace Commission on Managing in a Political Environment* London: SOLACE

Stanley M (2006) How to be a Civil Servant website see 'Accountability, Propriety, and Audit' see www.civilservant.org.uk

State Service Commission (2003) *The Relationship between the Public Service and Ministers* Fact Sheet No. 3, Wellington: State Service Commission

Stoker G (2006) 'Public Value Management: A New Narrative for Networked Governance?' in *The American Review of Public Administration 2006* 36: 41-57

Straw E (2004) *The Dead Generalist: Reforming the civil service and public services* London: Demos

Strategy Unit (2003a) *Innovation in the Public Sector* London: The Stationery Office

Strategy Unit (2003b) *Strategic Audit: Progress and Challenges for the UK* London: The Stationery Office

Talbot C (2004) 'Executive Agencies: Have they improved management in government?' in *Public Money & Management* Vol. 24, No. 2

Talbot C (2005) *The Future of the Civil Service* paper presented to the Public Management Policy Association

Times, The (2003; 2004; 2005) *The Times Top 100 Graduate Employers* London: Times

Theakston K (1995) *The Civil Service since 1945* London: Blackwell

Guardian, The (2005) 'Foreign Office amateurish and over-staffed, says report', 4 August

Thomson W (2006) 'To succeed you need to find strength beyond Whitehall' in Bichard M (ed) *A word in your ear ... Advice to Sir Gus from a friendly source* Solace Imprint Foundation: January 2006

Toynbee P (2006) 'Ministers have as much of a clue as you or me' *The Guardian*, 17 January

Treasury and Civil Service Select Committee (1986) *Civil Servants and ministers: duties and responsibilities* Session 1985-86 Seventh Report, Vol. I: HC 92-I

Treasury Select Committee (2001) *HM Treasury Third Report 2000-01* London: The Stationery Office

Turnbull A (2005) *Sir Andrew Turnbull's valedictory lecture*, available at www.civilservice.gov.uk/speeches/valedictory_lecture.asp

Turpin C (1994) 'Ministerial Responsibility' in Jowell J and Oliver D (eds) *The Changing Constitution* Third Edition, Oxford: OUP

Weir S and Beetham D (1999) *Political Power and Democratic Control in Britain* London: Routledge

Weller P and Young L (2001) 'Australia: mandarins or lemons?' in Rhodes RAW and Weller P (eds) *The Changing World of Top Officials* Buckingham: Open University

Woodhouse D (2002) 'The Reconstruction of the Constitutional Accountability' in *Public Law* Spring

Woodhouse D (2003) 'Ministerial Responsibility' in Bogdanor V (ed) *The British Constitution in the Twentieth Century* Oxford: OUP